bead stitching
HANDBOOK

Bead&BUTTON

MW01040643

Kalmbach
Media

Kalmbach Books
A division of Kalmbach Media
21027 Crossroads Circle
Waukesha, Wisconsin 53186
www.JewelryAndBeadingStore.com

© 2019 Kalmbach Books

All rights reserved. Except for brief excerpts for review, this book may not be reproduced in part or in whole by electronic means or otherwise without written permission of the publisher.

Photography © 2019 Kalmbach Books except where otherwise noted.

The jewelry designs in *Bead Stitching Handbook* are the copyrighted property of the author, and they may not be taught or sold without permission. Please use them for your education and personal enjoyment only.

Published in 2019
24 23 22 21 20   2 3 4 5 6

Manufactured in China

ISBN: 978-1-62700-553-1
EISBN: 978-1-62700-554-8

The material in this book has appeared previously in *Bead&Button* magazine. Bead&Button is registered as a trademark.

Editor: Erica Barse
Book Design: Lisa Bergman
Illustrator: Kellie Jaeger
Photographer: William Zuback

Library of Congress Control Number: 2018939848

bead
stitching
HANDBOOK

Introduction • 6

Basics • 7

Materials • 8
Thread and cord, beads, pearls, and crystals

Tools • 18
Pliers, cutters, and needles

Beading fundamentals • 20
Conditioning, knots, and wire loops

contents

stitches

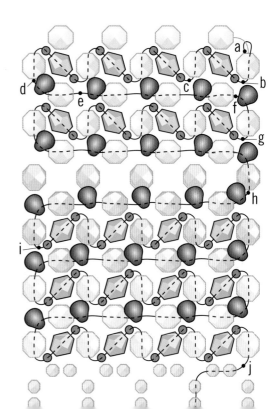

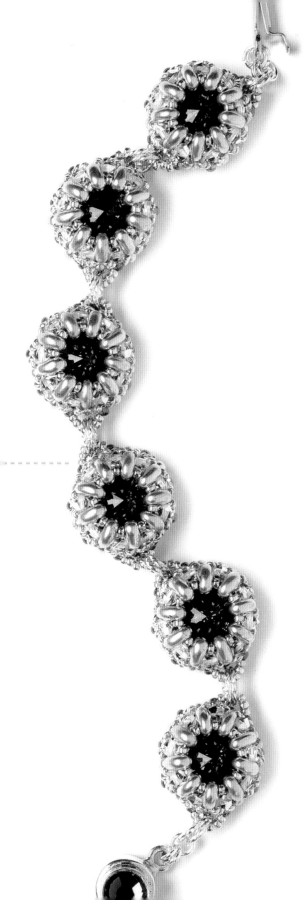

Projects • 71

introduction

Kalmbach Media is proud to present *The Bead Stitching Handbook*. The talented editors of *Bead&Button* magazine have collected all the information you need for successful bead stitching—in one handy volume. This book features 15 essential stitching techniques, information about the beads and tools you'll need to complete a new project, helpful tips for beading success, and 20 beautiful jewelry pieces to make and wear.

In this comprehensive guide to bead stitching, you'll find clear and complete instructions for your favorite stitches, such as peyote, herringbone, and right-angle weave—along with chenille stitch, chevron chain, bead crochet, loomwork, and more. Also included is a thorough discussion of the various supplies needed for detailed beadwork, such as crystals, pearls, and of course, seed beads of all sizes and shapes.

Once you've mastered the basics, you can stretch your beading skills by applying these stitches in the 20 step-by-step projects that follow. Ranging from beginner-friendly to advanced-intermediate, every design in this book has been editor-tested. You're sure to find a stitch or style to fit your taste.

We hope you enjoy this collection and use it as a reference in your everyday jewelry making for years to come.

Happy beading!

Erica Barse
Senior Editor
Kalmbach Books

basics

SEED BEADS

Shopping for beads can feel as complicated as high-school geometry. Cover all the angles with this handy guide to seed beads, shaped beads, and the myriad multi-hole beads that have been released.

SINGLE-HOLE SEED BEADS

ROUND: Don't be fooled by the name; round seed beads are not perfect spheres. They're more donut shaped, and their profile varies by manufacturer. Seed beads made by Japanese manufacturers Miyuki and Toho tend to be taller and have larger holes, while Czech-made versions are flatter with smaller holes. Round seed beads occasionally have square holes, and sometimes you'll see round seed beads called "rocailles."

CHARLOTTE: Traditionally, Charlottes are 13º round seed beads that have a single facet ground into the side to catch the light and dazzle the eye. Beads of other sizes are also made in this shape and are sometimes called "one-cuts" or "true-cuts."

DEMI BEADS: New from Toho in 2016, Demis are the same diameter as 11º and 8º seed beads, but only half the height.

CYLINDER: If you were to saw a long thin pipe into short segments, you'd have something like cylinder beads. At your local bead store, these tiny tube-shaped beads may be called Delicas (Miyuki-brand cylinders) or Treasures or Aikos (made by Toho).

HEX-CUT: As the name implies, these seed beads have six sides cut into them; look at them from the ends to see the hexagonal shape. And don't let this throw you: Czech-made hex-cuts are sometimes called "two-cuts."

THREE-CUT: Three-cut seed beads actually boast more than three facets; in fact, they have the most facets of any seed bead. The identifying facets are on the ends, tapering the bead toward the hole.

TRIANGLE: Triangle beads look like an equilateral triangle when viewed from the top. Toho triangles have sharp corners. Miyuki makes triangles with either rounded corners or sharp corners (called "sharp triangles").

CUBE: Cube beads are three-dimensional squares, but certain details depend on the manufacturer. Miyuki cube beads have slightly sharper corners; the Toho variety are more rounded. Cube beads may also be called "squares" but should not be confused with flat squares, such as the two-hole Tila and tile beads.

DROP: Drop beads are pear shaped with the hole going through the top horizontally. Drops are also called "teardrops," and since they are frequently used in fringe, you may also see them labeled as "fringe drops" or "fringe beads." They are closely related to magatamas and are sometimes referred to as such, but there is a difference.

MAGATAMA: Magatamas look like squashed drop beads with the hole just off center. Once you can tell a magatama from a drop, make sure to learn the difference between a magatama and a long magatama (a much clearer distinction).

LONG MAGATAMA: When viewed from the front, long or "elongated" magatamas look like stretched-out magatamas. But from the side, you see an angled profile as the bottom of each bead slants away from the top.

BUGLES: Bugle beads are basically long cylinder beads. Bugles can be smooth, twisted, spiral, hex-cut, square, or triangular in shape, and have round or square holes.

DAGGER: In the same family as drops and magatamas, dagger beads look like sword blades or flower petals. Their shape puts them on the larger end of the seed bead spectrum. Half daggers are also available.

PEANUT: This shape goes by many descriptors depending on the manufacturer or distributor, the most common being farfalle (like the pasta), bowtie, butterfly, dogbone, and berry. Whatever you call it, this bead has two rounded ends joined by a short, thin middle where the hole is. Although most peanut beads are about the same size, Miyuki's "berry beads" have a slightly thicker middle than other brands.

TIP A flurry of two-hole and multi-hole seed beads are available today. This roundup is organized by general shape so you can easily see which ones might have potential for substitutions or combinations.

OVAL/PINCHED OVAL

SuperDuo: 2.5 x 5 mm oval that is slightly pinched at each end

MiniDuo: 2 x 4 mm oval; a smaller version of the SuperDuo

Twin: 2.5 x 5 mm oval bead with two holes

Pressed Twin: 2.5 x 5 mm oval that is slightly pinched at each end

Super8: 2 x 4.7 mm oval-ish with pinched ends

SQUARE/TILE

Tila: 5 mm tile with two parallel holes

Tile: 6 mm tile with two parallel holes

QuadraTile: 6 mm tile with four holes through the face of the bead

Chexx: 6 mm tile with two holes through the face of the bead

Silky: 6 mm tile with two holes that go through opposite corners

Crisscross cube: 4 mm cube with offset holes that cross through the cube

RECTANGLE

Bar: 2 x 6 mm slim, rounded rectangle with two holes

Brick: 3 x 6 mm rectangle with two holes

Half Tila: 2.5 x 5 mm rectangle with two holes

CYLINDER

Rulla: 3 x 5 mm cylinder with two holes

Twin roller: 3.5 x 9 mm capsule with two holes

ROUND/DISK

QuadraLentil: 6 mm disk with four holes

Lentil: 6 mm disk with two holes

Piggy bead: 8 mm curved disk with one center and one offset hole

RounDuo: 5 mm sphere with two parallel holes

DiscDuo: 6 mm flat, disk-shaped bead with two holes

TRIANGLE

Triangle: 6 mm equilateral triangle with two holes on one side

Kheops: 6 mm equilateral triangle with two holes running base to tip

Tango: 6 mm right triangle with holes through the point and the base

eMMA: 3 x 6 mm equilateral triangle with three holes through face

Trinity beads: 6 and 8 mm rounded triangles with three holes

OTHER SHAPES

Chilli: 4 x 11 mm cupped, elongated drop with two holes

Crescent: 3 x 10 mm crescent shape with two holes spaced 3 mm apart

Daggers: 5 x 16 mm elongated spear / drop with two holes at the narrow end

Honeycomb: 6 mm hexagon with two parallel holes

Infinity: 3 x 6 mm infinity or figure-eight shape with two holes

Pyramid hex: 12 mm hexagonal pyramid with flat bottom and two holes

Stud: 8 or 12 mm square pyramid with flat bottom and two holes

Tipp bead: 8 mm cone with flat bottom and two holes

Zorro: 6 x 5 mm Z-shaped bead with two holes

Arcos and Minos beads: Two separate beads that were designed to work together, the Arcos bead is a 5 x 10 mm crescent shape with three holes and an even thickness; the Minos bead is a 2.5 x 3 mm cylinder that fits perfectly within the center of two Arcos beads

DiamonDuos: 5 x 8 mm diamond shape with a hole at each end; one side is flat, and the other has a raised center that looks like facets

SEED BEAD FINISHES

Seed beads come in a dizzying array of colors and styles. While sometimes it's enough to just like a particular color, arming yourself with more information may help prevent some unpleasant surprises. Below is a guide to the different glass types used to make seed beads and some of the various finishes that you may find.

GLASS TYPE

Transparent: Clear or colored glass that transmits light

Opaque: Colored glass that does not transmit light

Color-lined: Colored or clear transparent glass and has an opaque colored lining on the inside

Metal-lined: Clear or colored transparent glass with a core of real metal or metallic-colored paint. The metallic lining gives these beads extra sparkle. Some have a square hole, which increases the sparkle.

Metallic: A baked-on paint or electroplated finish resembling metal. Many are stable, but some wear off over time. To test for permanence, soak them in bleach or acetone. To prolong the life of the finish, spray the beads with an acrylic fixative such as Krylon (test first to make sure the fixative doesn't affect the color of the beads).

FINISH

AB: An iridescent finish resembling an oil slick; sometimes called iris, rainbow, or aurora borealis.

Luster: A transparent glaze that lends extra sparkle.

Matte: An etched surface with a velvety, frosted look.

Matte AB: A matte finish with an AB coating, resulting in a soft, variegated look.

Semi-matte: A slightly etched surface with a silky finish.

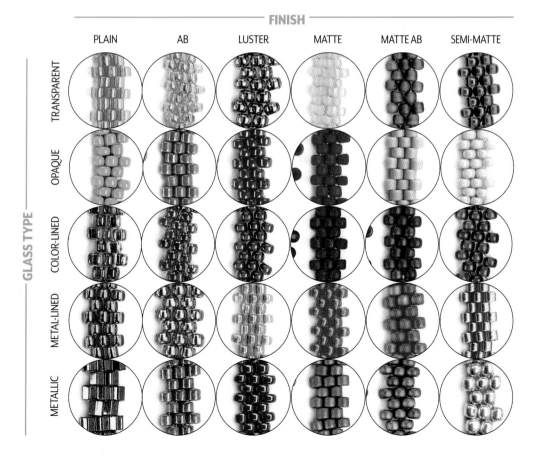

	FINISH					
GLASS TYPE	PLAIN	AB	LUSTER	MATTE	MATTE AB	SEMI-MATTE
TRANSPARENT						
OPAQUE						
COLOR-LINED						
METAL-LINED						
METALLIC						

Special finishes

Galvanized beads, traditionally, are coated with a zinc-based finish which rubs off easily and should be coated with a fixative to prolong the life of the beads. The new Duracoat (Miyuki) and Permanent Finish Galvanized (Toho) beads are much more stable.

Metal-plated beads are plated with a thin coating of metal such as high-karat gold, sterling silver, copper, titanium, palladium, or nickel. This is a permanent finish, though the metal layer may wear off over time.

Pearl refers to a lustrous, pearly finish on an opaque bead.

Opal beads have a milky, semi-translucent finish. Some are gilt-lined.

White hearts are dark transparent or opaque beads with an opaque white core.

Striped beads are made with two or more colors of glass in a striped pattern.

Ceylon refers to a lustrous, pearly finish on a semi-transparent bead.

Satin beads have a striated appearance.

Two-tone beads are made with two colors of glass.

Gold luster refers to a luster finish with glowing gold highlights.

Painted or dyed beads have an impermanent color coating. Many bright purples, pinks, and fuchsias are painted or dyed. Exposure to sunlight will cause the colors to fade, and the colorants may rub off when handled.

TIP Sometimes seed beads may flake or tarnish once they're exposed to the oils on your skin. In order to combat this, try coating your beads with clear nail polish to help maintain their finish.

SEED BEADS PER GRAM

Knowing how many individual beads you need is only marginally helpful when talking about seed beads, which are usually sold in tubes or packages of anywhere from 7 to 40 grams or more. Here in the U.S., however, most of us don't have a clue as to what constitutes a gram. The topic is further complicated by factors such as style variances between manufacturers and finishes and linings that sometimes add a marginal amount of weight to each bead. (And this just refers to non-metallic finishes; see the tip, below, to learn about metallics.)

ROUND SEED BEADS

Size	Amount per gram
6°	10–20
8°	40–55
11°	120–150
15°	300–350

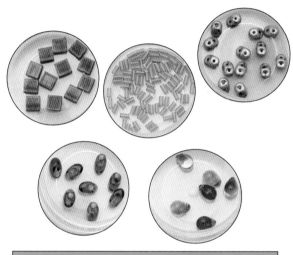

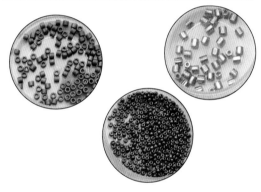

SHAPED SEED BEADS

Size	Shape	Amount per gram
3 mm	Bugle	90–100
6 mm	Bugle	25–35
5°	Triangle	10–12
11°	Triangle	80–90
1.5 mm	Cube	100–110
3 mm	Cube	15–20
3–4 mm	Fringe drop	20–25
6–7 mm	Fringe drop	5–6
3–4 mm	Magatama	14–16
4 x 7 mm	Long magatama	8–12
2 x 4 mm	Peanut/Berry/Farfalle	35–40
5 mm	Tila	10–14
6 mm	CzechMates tile	6–7
2.5 x 5 mm	Twin	16–18
2.5 x 5 mm	SuperDuo	16–18

CYLINDERS & CUT SEED BEADS

Size	Cut	Amount per gram
8°	Hex/two-cut	40–50
10°	Cylinder	110–120
11°	Cylinder	200–220
13°	Charlotte/one-cut	300–350

TIP Different finishes and linings affect the weight of a bead slightly. Metallic finishes add a more noticeable weight to each bead, so there will be fewer beads in one gram. For instance, there are 120–150 non-metallic round 11° seed beads in one gram but only 110–130 of their metallic counterparts. When purchasing metallic seed beads for a project that uses non-metallic beads, you may want to buy more than what is called for in the materials list.

CRYSTALS

Crystals come in many different shapes, sizes, colors, and finishes.

Glass beads are composed of sand (silica), soda ash (sodium carbonate), and limestone (calcium carbonate), and crystals are made of the same stuff with the addition of lead. Lead makes crystals clear and allows light to really reflect inside the beads. Lead also makes crystals heavier than glass beads. Crystal beads do not come from naturally occurring crystalline minerals; crystals are manufactured, not mined. "Lead," "leaded," or "full-lead" crystals must have a chemical makeup of at least 24 percent lead, while beads with less lead are just called "crystals." Occasionally, you will see lead-free glass beads called crystals because they are faceted like their leaded counterparts, but these are not true crystals.

MANUFACTURERS

Swarovski: Swarovski is a huge name in the industry; you may hear their product referred to as Austrian crystal, as it's made in Wattens, Austria. With a minimum of 32 percent lead and a ridiculous number of facets, Swarovski crystals are crisp, clear, and ultra-sparkly. These crystals are usually the most expensive.

Preciosa: Based in Jablonec nad Nisou in Northern Bohemia, Preciosa is the premier manufacturer of Czech crystal. Their products contain about 30 percent lead and get kudos for superior cut and clarity. They're more affordable.

Chinese crystal: Artisans have been making crystal in Austria and Bohemia for centuries, so it's not surprising that a few brands have distinguished themselves. In China, crystal production is a more recent development, so there are many brands to choose from, such as Thunder Polish. Chinese crystals have considerably less lead and are the most cost-effective around, although the beads will not be as precisely shaped.

SHAPES AND SIZES

Xilion is the name given to Swarovski's latest take on the bicone. Like the name suggests, bicones look like two conical shapes attached at the base. Across manufacturers, the bicone is right up there with round crystals as the most popular shape. You'll also find crystal cubes, teardrops, briolettes, ovals, and rondelles. Crystal pendants come in all kinds of specialty shapes, like hearts, butterflies, leaves, flowers, rings, and abstract shapes. Also, components such as crystal buttons, sew-on stones, sequins, flat-backs, and crystal-studded beads and findings, like clasps, head pins, and chain are available.

A rivoli is a round crystal stone that is pointed on both the front and the back. A dentelle, on the other hand, is a round crystal stone with a pointed back and a faceted front that does not come to a point. A chaton has a flat back and a faceted front that, like a dentelle, does not come to a point. Other crystal stone shapes include baguettes (rectangles) and navettes (ovals).

Crystal stones may be measured in millimeters or by stone size (SS). Crystal products range from the miniscule 2 mm round crystal bead to pendants nearly 40 mm in length.

Size comparison

SS5	1.7–1.8 mm
SS6	2–2.1 mm
SS8	2.4–2.5 mm
SS12	3–3.2 mm
SS14	3.5–3.6 mm
SS17	4–4.1 mm
SS18	4.2–4.4 mm
SS19	4.4–4.6 mm
SS24	5.27–5.44 mm
SS29	6.14–6.32 mm

SPECIAL FINISHES

There's often an abbreviation tacked onto the end to indicate any special-effect finishes. Usually only one half of a crystal receives a finish; 2X means that both halves have been treated. AB translates to Aurora Borealis, a reflective iridescent finish, while CAL stands for Comet Argent Light, a silvery sheen. Not all finishes are abbreviated (satin, vitrail, and arum, to name a few).

Crystal pearls

To make crystal pearls, manufacturers take a round crystal bead and build up a man-made pearlescent coating around it. The result is a perfectly round faux pearl with the weight of the real deal.

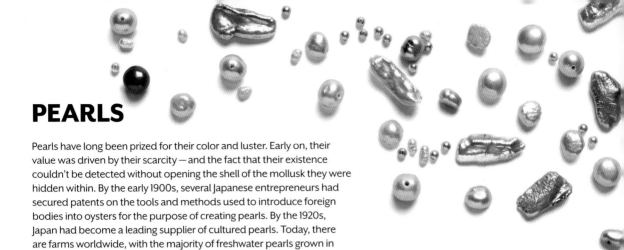

PEARLS

Pearls have long been prized for their color and luster. Early on, their value was driven by their scarcity — and the fact that their existence couldn't be detected without opening the shell of the mollusk they were hidden within. By the early 1900s, several Japanese entrepreneurs had secured patents on the tools and methods used to introduce foreign bodies into oysters for the purpose of creating pearls. By the 1920s, Japan had become a leading supplier of cultured pearls. Today, there are farms worldwide, with the majority of freshwater pearls grown in China. A mussel can produce several dozen pearls in one harvest season while a saltwater oyster may only produce one or two pearls in the same amount of time.

Cultured pearls are the standard today with natural pearls showing up mainly in vintage jewelry. Naturally-colored pinks are the most expensive, followed by white, light cream, cream, dark cream, and yellow. As organic material, both saltwater and freshwater pearls are susceptible to water temperature ranges and cosmetics, hair products, and other chemicals.

TYPES, RANGING FROM MOST TO LEAST EXPENSIVE

Akoya: Harvested in saltwater oysters off the coast of Japan. Round, white with rose glow. Known for their high-quality luster.

South Sea: Exceptional quality, prized for smoothness and roundness; cultivation in the large oysters is difficult. Expensive because this oyster is sensitive to the culturing process. White, cream, golden.

Tahitian: Expensive because this oyster is sensitive to the culturing process. Ranges from metallic silver to black.

Abalone: Not really pearls, but formed in abalone shells. Cannot be cultured due to the fragility of the abalone. Mabes (half-pearls) typically used in jewelry making. Iridescent, metallic colors ranging from silver to greens and blues.

Keshi: Japanese for "tiny." Rejected by oysters before the end of the culturing process. Solid nacre but as a by-product of the culturing process, not considered natural. Many colors including traditional pearl colors ranging from white to cream and rose. High luster, random, freeform shapes.

Mabe: Half pearls that grow on the side of the shell and are cut off and backed with mother of pearl. Solid white, cream, pink, blue and rainbow-hued. Pink with gold swirls are very valuable.

Crystal: Made with crystal base and powder-coated and painted; perfume- and chemical-resistant. Dozens of shapes and sizes; colors are standard and don't vary between lots; colors won't fade.

Glass: Durable, scratch-resistant. Don't last as long as crystal pearls, scratch and fade more easily.

Plastic: Not scratch-resistant; very cost-effective; standard shapes. Colors fade over time.

American Gem Trade Association designations

Learn these terms to help you identify any treatment your pearls may have undergone.

Natural: not enhanced
Bleached: color removed or lightened with heat, light, or other agents
Dyed: introduction of coloring matter to add a new color, intensify color, or improve color uniformity
Irradiated: color altered by the use of neutrons, gamma rays, or beta particles

THREAD AND CORD

The unsung hero of beading, thread is as vital to beading as are beads, and choosing the right one for your project can be the difference between success and failure. A wide variety of threads are available for beading, and many that were originally intended for something else – such as upholstery, tailoring, and fishing – are now being marketed specifically to beaders. The majority of the choices fall into one of two camps – nylon threads and gel-spun polyethylene (GSP, Dynema, and Spectra Fiber are some names this product is marketed under) – though some other products are available as well.

Thread choice is highly subjective. No single thread is perfect for all beading applications and every beader has favorites. Factors that will influence your thread choice include beads used in the project, stitch type, and handling preferences. For instance, if your beads have sharp edges, as do bugles and crystals, you may want to use a thread that is very strong and resists fraying. If you're loom weaving, you may want to warp your loom with thread that doesn't stretch so as to prevent your work from buckling. If you want the piece to be very fluid, rather than stiff, you'll want to choose a thin, silky thread that will give your beadwork a lot of drape.

NYLON THREADS

Nylon threads are available either as parallel filament fibers or plied fibers. Parallel fibers are strong and usually flat, making them easy to thread through the eye of a beading needle. The plied fibers are round, making them more difficult to thread through a needle. Plied fibers are incredibly strong, however, so many people cope with threading challenges either by using a different kind of needle, or devising methods to making threading easier. Most (but not all) nylon threads stretch, and will benefit from having some stretch pulled out of it before you begin stitching. Some are pre-waxed or bonded to resist fraying and reduce wear. Those that are not will benefit from a coating of beeswax or thread conditioner before stitching. Nylon threads come in a multitude of colors, so it's easy to find a thread to match almost any project you undertake. Nylon threads are sized with either a letter or a number. For those with letter designations, the closer to the beginning of the alphabet, the thinner the thread, except in the case of size O, OO, or OOO, which are the thinnest threads available. For those that are numbered, the smaller the number, the thinner the thread. Nylon upholstery thread can be used for beading, but as it is thicker than most other nylon threads, it may be best for bead crochet.

GSP

Gel-spun polyethylene is a polymer fiber originally developed for the fishing industry. As such, these fibers are designed to break down in sunlight over time. However, unless you plan on leaving your beadwork in a sunny window, these fibers are generally safe to use for beadwork. Also available in both plied and parallel varieties, GSP products are extremely strong and fray-resistant. They do not stretch, so the tension in your beadwork cannot be adjusted. As with nylon, some GSP fibers are coated for additional strength and smoothness. Because it comes from the fishing industry, the size is usually given in diameter (e.g. .008 in.) and/or breaking strength (e.g. 6 lb. test). Each product has slightly different characteristics, but in general, they're very good for making strong beadwork. The major downside to GSP fibers is the limited color palette, as these products are only available in black, gray, white, and moss green.

OTHER PRODUCTS

The other notable thread options are Aramid, the fiber that bullet-proof vests are made from, and polyester. Aramid, sold under the brand name Kevlar, is extremely strong, fray resistant, and heat tolerant, but it has one major drawback: it will cut itself if two pieces cross each other under tension. Therefore, it shouldn't be used in certain stitches, like double helix, and you must be very careful about knots (supposedly surgeon's knots are OK). The natural color of Aramid is yellow, but it can be dyed other colors with fabric dyes.

Polyester thread can also be used for beading, though it is a bit thicker than many other available threads. You can find polyester thread in fabric stores. Look for sewing, quilting, or buttonhole thread.

Do not use cotton thread for beading. It is too weak and will rot over time.

Size Equivalents

Thread	Cord	GSP
00	–	6 lb. parallel
A/0	–	8 lb. parallel
B	–	10 lb. parallel
D	0	10–15 lb. plied
E	1	20 lb. plied
F	2	30 lb. plied
FF	3	–

BEADING TOOLS

You can find beading tools for almost any task imaginable, but the basics fall under three categories: pliers, cutters, and needles. For most bead stitching, you can get by with a minimum of tools. As you gain more experience, you'll find that a wide range of specialty tools can help you save time and improve the quality of your work.

PLIERS

Pliers are used for holding, bending, and shaping wire and for opening and closing loops and jump rings.

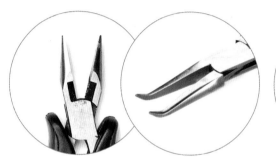

Chainnose pliers have flat jaws used to bend and shape wire and open and close jump rings.

Closely related to chainnose pliers are **flatnose and bentnose pliers**. Like chainnose pliers, these tools have smooth inner jaws to help you grasp wire or components without leaving marks. Their specialized shapes help you get a comfortable grip on narrow or awkward spaces.

Roundnose pliers have round jaws that taper to a point. They are used to shape wire and form loops.

CUTTERS

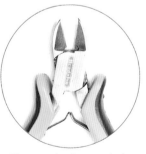

Crimping pliers are used to crimp beads and flexible beading wire. They compress tube crimps into narrow cylinders that hold strung projects in place. To learn more about crimping, see p. 21.

Nylon-jaw pliers have a protective layer on the jaws, which keeps them from marking soft metal or wire. They can be used to hold pieces while you work with other pliers, or for straightening wire.

The most basic cutter is the **diagonal wire cutter**, used to trim flexible beading wire and narrow gauges of wire to the desired length. As the name implies, these cutters trim the wire at an angle, leaving a point at the tip of the wire.

A small, sharp pair of **scissors** is a must-have for beadwork. It's best to use these scissors only for beadwork to maintain their sharp edge.

NEEDLES

Beading needles are essential for successful stitching. The smaller the needle, the bigger the needle number. To choose a needle, consider your bead and thread sizes, the number of passes you'll make through the beads, and the beading techniques used.

NEEDLE SIZES

Big Eye
Use for loomwork or transferring beads (for bead crochet and kumihimo).

Small Big Eye
Use for off-loom stitches, getting through tight spots, and transferring beads.

Twisted wire
Use for stringing and getting through tight spots.

#12 long
Use for loomwork, off-loom stitches, and transferring beads.

#10
Use with 6° to 11° seed beads.

#12
Use with 8° to 13° seed beads.

#13
Use with 11° to 15° seed beads.

#16
Use with 16° to 24° seed beads.

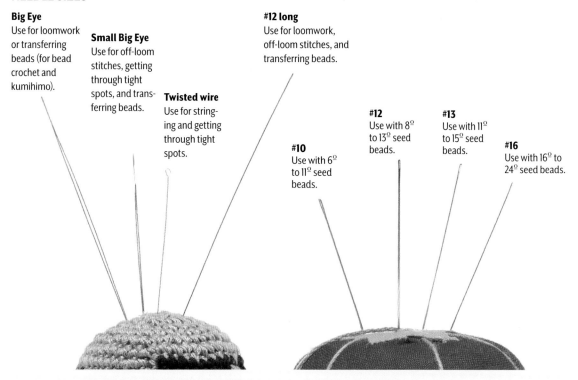

Threading a needle

Threading the narrow eye of a beading needle can be tricky. Try these tips for success.

1 Cut the thread, hold one end in each hand, and pull. If you're working with Nymo, condition it. This relaxes the thread's kinks and curls, making it easier to use.
2 Trim the end of your thread on an angle using very sharp scissors. A tapered edge free of stray fibers will slide gracefully through the needle's eye.
3 Flatten the thread's cut edge to its thinnest profile by pressing it with your fingernails, squeezing it with pliers, or biting it gently with your teeth.
4 Hold the needle in your dominant hand, and grab the thread close to the cut edge with your other hand. Move the needle to the thread, sliding the eye over the thread's end **(photo)**.
5 Pass the wire loop of a needle threader through the eye of your needle. Put your thread through the loop, then pull the loop out of the needle.

BEADING FUNDAMENTALS

A handful of techniques show up in project after project, so we consider them to be fundamental skills. Mastering these skills will help you create long-lasting, sturdy beadwork that will last a lifetime, so be sure to practice any of these techniques that are unfamiliar.

CONDITIONING THREAD

Use wax (beeswax or microcrystalline wax) or a thread conditioner (like Thread Heaven or Thread Magic), to condition nylon beading thread and Fireline. Wax smooths nylon fibers and adds tackiness that will stiffen your beadwork slightly. Conditioners add a static charge that causes the thread to repel itself, so don't use it with doubled thread. To condition, stretch nylon thread to remove the curl (you don't need to stretch Fireline). Place the thread or Fireline on top of the conditioner, hold it in place with your thumb or finger, and pull the thread through the conditioner.

ENDING AND ADDING THREAD

To end a thread: Sew back through the last few rows or rounds of beadwork, following the thread path of the stitch and tying two or three half-hitch knots (see "Half-hitch knot") between beads as you go. Sew through a few beads after the last knot, and trim the thread.

To add a thread: Sew into the beadwork several rows or rounds prior to the point where the last bead was added, leaving a short tail. Follow the thread path of the stitch, tying a few half-hitch knots between beads as you go, and exit where the last stitch ended. Trim the short tail.

 Many beading projects call for a product called Fireline, which is a super-tough fishing line. While regular scissors or wire cutters will work fine for most threads, they usually won't cut through Fireline easily. Luckily, there are a handful of products that do the job with ease. Try these to find your favorite:
- **Xuron Fireline Cutters**
- **Chikamasa scissors**
- **The Snip by Boomerang Tool Company**
- **Fiskars Kids' Scissors**

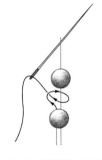

HALF-HITCH KNOT

Pass the needle under the thread bridge between two beads, and pull gently until a loop forms. Sew through the loop, and pull gently to draw the knot into the beadwork.

OVERHAND KNOT

Make a loop with the thread. Pull the tail through the loop, and tighten.

SQUARE KNOT

1 Cross one end of the thread over and under the other end. Pull both ends to tighten the first half of the knot.
2 Cross the first end of the thread over and under the other end. Pull both ends to tighten the knot.

SURGEON'S KNOT

Cross the left-hand end of the thread over the right twice. Pull to tighten. Cross the end that is now on the right over the left, go through the loop, and tighten.

ATTACHING A STOP BEAD

Use a stop bead to secure beads temporarily when you begin stitching: Pick up the stop bead, leaving the desired length tail. Sew through the stop bead again in the same direction, making sure you don't split the thread inside the bead. Sew through the bead one more time for added security.

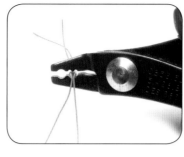

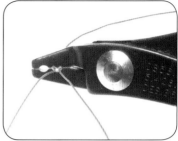

CRIMPING

Use a crimp bead to secure two ends of beading wire. Slide the crimp bead into place, and squeeze it firmly with chainnose pliers to flatten it. Or, for a more finished look, use crimping pliers:

1 Position the crimp bead in the hole that is closest to the handle of the crimping pliers.

2 Holding the wires apart, squeeze the pliers to compress the crimp bead, making sure one wire is on each side of the dent.

3 Place the crimp bead in the front hole of the pliers, and position it so the dent is facing the tips of the pliers. Squeeze the pliers to fold the crimp in half.

4 Tug on the wires to ensure that the crimp bead is secure.

OPENING AND CLOSING LOOPS AND JUMP RINGS

1 Hold a loop or a jump ring with two pairs of pliers, such as chainnose, flatnose, or bentnose pliers.

2 To open the loop or jump ring, bring the tips of one pair of pliers toward you, and push the tips of the other pair away from you.

3 Reverse step 2 to close the open loop or jump ring.

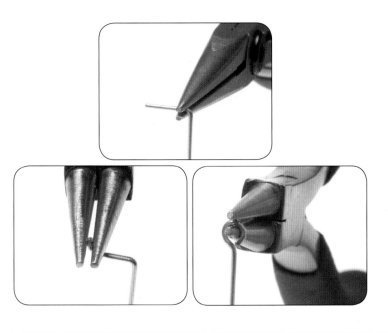

PLAIN LOOP

1 Using chainnose pliers, make a right-angle bend in the wire directly above a bead or other component or at least ¼ in. (6 mm) from the end of a piece of wire. For a larger loop, bend the wire farther in.

2 Grip the end of the wire with roundnose pliers so that the wire is flush with the jaws of the pliers where they meet. The closer to the tip of the pliers that you work, the smaller the loop will be. Press downward slightly, and rotate the wire toward the bend made in step 1.

3 Reposition the pliers in the loop to continue rotating the wire until the end of the wire touches the bend.

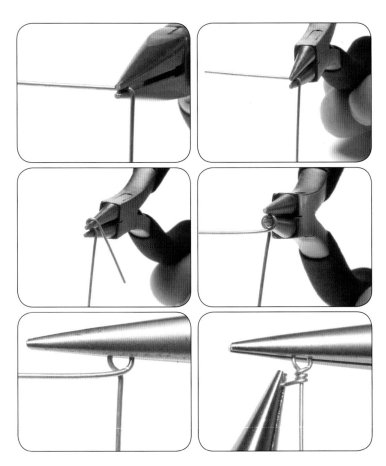

WRAPPED LOOP

1 Using chainnose pliers, make a right-angle bend in the wire about 2 mm above a bead or other component or at least 1¼ in. (3.2 cm) from the end of a piece of wire.

2 Position the jaws of the roundnose pliers in the bend. The closer to the tip of the pliers that you work, the smaller the loop will be.

3 Curve the short end of the wire over the top jaw of the roundnose pliers.

4 Reposition the pliers so the lower jaw fits snugly in the loop. Curve the wire downward around the bottom jaw of the pliers. This is the first half of a wrapped loop.

5 To complete the wraps, grasp the top of the loop with one pair of pliers.

6 With another pair of pliers, wrap the wire around the stem two or three times. Trim the excess wire, and gently press the cut end close to the wraps with chainnose pliers.

stitches

PEYOTE BASICS

The perfect technique for both flat bands and structural shapes, peyote stitch is wonderfully versatile. Regardless of the variation, all peyote techniques are based on the same basic thread path, which causes offset rows of beads to nestle together. If you're a beginner, start with "Peyote basics." Try a few easy projects with these skills, and then move on to the "Shaping" and "Advanced techniques." To learn to make peyote bezels, see p. 32.

MATERIALS

samples
- assorted 15º–5º seed beads
- Fireline, 6 lb. test, or nylon beading thread, size D
- beading needles, #12

TECHNIQUES
- beading fundamentals: attaching a stop bead, square knot (p. 20)

FLAT PEYOTE

Learn the most basic form of peyote.

FLAT EVEN-COUNT

The term "even-count peyote stitch" means that there are an even number of beads in each row.

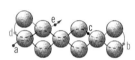

1 Thread a needle on a comfortable length of thread, and attach a stop bead about 6 in. (15 cm) from the end. The stop bead isn't absolutely necessary, but it will prevent your beads from sliding off the thread, and it will also help you maintain good tension while you're stitching. Pick up an even number of beads (**figure, a–b**). These beads will shift to form rows 1 and 2 as row 3 is added.

2 To begin row 3, pick up a bead, skip the last bead strung in the previous step, and sew back through the next bead in the opposite direction (**b–c**). Position the new bead to sit next to the bead you skipped, so their holes are parallel. For each subsequent stitch in the row, pick up a bead, skip a bead in the previous step, and sew through the next bead, until your thread exits the first bead strung (**c–d**). The beads added in this row stick out from the previous beads and are referred to as "up-beads."

3 For each stitch in subsequent rows, pick up a bead, and sew through the next up-bead in the previous row (**d–e**).

Getting started

If you're struggling with the first few rows, try one of these three methods:
- After stringing the beads for rows 1 and 2, pinch the beads between your thumb and forefinger. Pick up the first bead for row 3, skip the end bead, and sew back through the previous bead (**photo a**). Continue holding the beads in place as you complete the row (**photo b**).
- If the pinch method doesn't work for you, try passing a wire, pin, or needle through every other bead in the first strand (**photo c**). This creates the peyote alignment, making it easier for you to see which beads to sew through in the next row.
- Another option is to use a Quick Start Peyote card. These durable, laminated cards have openings to hold the beads in row 1, turning them into up-beads from the start (**photo d**). This makes it a cinch to add subsequent rows. Get them at www.quickstartpeyote.com.

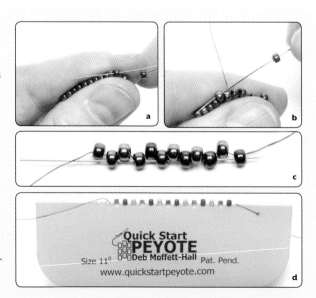

note Is your beadwork twisty and loose after working row 3, as in the top photo? Not to worry! Simply pull the working thread taut, pressing your thumbnail against the end bead to get the rows to straighten out.

FLAT ODD-COUNT

Flat odd-count peyote stitch has an odd number of beads in every other row. It is worked with the same thread path as even-count peyote, except for the turn after odd-numbered rows, where the last bead of the row can't be attached in the usual way because there is no up-bead to sew through. Begin an odd-count piece as follows:
1 Pick up an odd number of beads. Work row 3 as in even-count peyote, stopping before adding the last bead.
2 Work a figure-8 turn at the end of row 3: Sew through the first bead picked up in step 1 (bead #1). Pick up the last bead of the odd-numbered row (bead #8), and sew through beads #2, #3, #7, #2, #1, and #8 (**figure 1**).
3 Work row 4 as in even-count peyote, and then work row 5, stopping before adding the last bead.
4 In this and all subsequent odd-numbered rows, work the following turn: Pick up the last bead of the row, and then sew under the edge thread bridge immediately below. Sew back through the last bead added to begin the next row (**figure 2**).

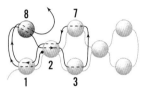

FIGURE 1

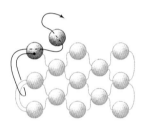

FIGURE 2

TWO-DROP PEYOTE STITCH

Work two-drop peyote stitch the same way as basic flat peyote, but treat pairs of beads as if they were single beads.
1 To work in even-count two-drop peyote, pick up an even number of beads that is divisible by four. To work in odd-count two-drop peyote, pick up an even number of beads that is not divisible by four. Remember, these beads will shift to form rows 1 and 2 as row 3 is added (**figure 1**).
2 To begin row 3, pick up two beads, skip two beads added in step 1, and sew back through the next two beads. Repeat this stitch across the row (**figure 2**).
3 If you are working in even-count two-drop peyote, you will not need to do anything special to turn and begin subsequent rows. If you are working in odd-count two-drop peyote, modify the turns as in steps 2 and 4 of "Flat odd-count peyote."

FIGURE 1

FIGURE 2

notes Yes, you can do three-drop peyote or four-drop or five-drop or ... you get the picture. If you want your piece to be even-count, make sure the total number of beads you pick up for the first two rows is divisible by two and the number of beads you want in each "drop."

You can also mix counts in a piece, so you might have a row that has a stitch with one bead, a stitch with two beads, and a stitch with three beads. See what kinds of interesting patterns and textures you can create just by playing around with bead counts!

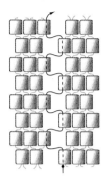

ZIPPING UP OR JOINING

To join two sections of a peyote piece invisibly, match up the two sections so the end rows fit together like puzzle pieces. If the end rows don't fit together, add or remove one row of peyote from either section. Then "zip up" the sections by zigzagging through the up-beads on both ends.

note Zigzag back through the beadwork to complete the join, making sure you connect the end beads on each edge.

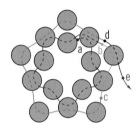

FIGURE 1

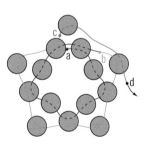

FIGURE 2

TUBULAR PEYOTE STITCH

Tubular peyote stitch follows the same stitching pattern as basic flat peyote, but instead of sewing back and forth, you work in rounds to form a tube.

TUBULAR EVEN-COUNT

1 Pick up an even number of beads to equal the desired circumference. Tie the beads into a ring with a square knot, leaving some slack between the beads, and sew through the first bead after the knot (**figure 1, a–b**). These beads will shift to form rounds 1 and 2 as round 3 is added.

2 Put the ring over a form if desired. To begin round 3, pick up a bead, skip the next bead in the ring, and sew through the following bead (**b–c**). Repeat this stitch to complete the round (**c–d**), and "step up" by sewing through the first up-bead added in this round (**d–e**). Stepping up positions your thread to begin the next round.

3 To work subsequent rounds, pick up a bead, and sew through the next up-bead in the previous round. Repeat this stitch to complete the round, and step up.

4 Repeat step 3 to the desired length.

TUBULAR ODD-COUNT

In odd-count tubular peyote, you don't need to step up; the beads will automatically form a continuous spiral.

1 Pick up an odd number of beads, tie them into a ring with a square knot, and sew through the first bead again (**figure 2, a–b**). These beads will shift to form rounds 1 and 2 as round 3 is added.

2 Work round 3 in tubular peyote stitch until you sew through the bead prior to the first bead in the ring (**b–c**). Pick up a bead, and sew through the next up-bead (**c–d**).

3 For subsequent rounds, continue working in tubular peyote, always sewing through the next up-bead.

CIRCULAR PEYOTE STITCH

Circular peyote stitch is worked in rounds like tubular peyote, but the rounds stay flat and radiate outward from the center as a result of incorporating increase stitches or larger beads in subsequent rounds.

TIP Count your rows. In peyote stitch, the beads nestle together, so to figure out how many rows or rounds you've stitched, identify a diagonal line of beads, and count how many there are in the diagonal line.

Make striped patterns

• To begin a tube with spiral stripes, alternate pairs of beads in each of two colors in the original ring. For subsequent rounds, pick up a bead of the opposite color as the bead directly below it for each stitch in the round.

• For **vertical stripes**, begin with a ring of beads that alternates color with every other bead. For subsequent rounds, pick up a bead of the same color as the bead directly below it for each stitch in the round.

• For **horizontal stripes**, start with a ring of beads in a single color. Work two or more rounds in the same color, depending on the desired width of the stripe, and then switch to a second color for the next two or more rounds. Alternate colors for the desired length.

• Combine these techniques to create a tube of all three kinds of stripes.

SHAPING

You can use peyote stitch to create wonderful shapes by increasing and decreasing your row count.

INCREASING AND DECREASING AT EDGES

EVEN-COUNT INCREASE

To increase one row along the edge when working in flat even-count peyote, pick up two beads, and sew through them again. Continue in the opposite direction to stitch the new row (**figure 1**).

EVEN-COUNT DECREASE

To decrease one row along the edge when working in flat even-count peyote, sew under the nearest thread bridge along the edge, and sew back through the last two beads you just sewed through (**figure 2**).

ODD-COUNT INCREASE

To increase one row along the edge when working in flat odd-count peyote, pick up the final bead for the row you're finishing, and sew through the adjacent bead and the bead just added. Pick up two beads, and sew back through the first bead added (**figure 3**).

ODD-COUNT DECREASE

To decrease one row along the edge when working in flat odd-count peyote, omit the final stitch in the row. Pick up a bead to begin the next row, and sew back through the last up-bead in the previous row (**figure 4**).

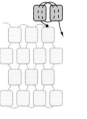

FIGURE 1   FIGURE 2

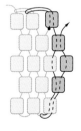
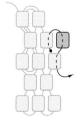

FIGURE 3   FIGURE 4

FIGURE 1

FIGURE 2

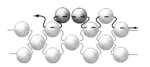

FIGURE 3

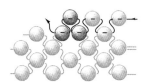

FIGURE 4

DECREASING AND INCREASING WITHIN A PIECE

DECREASING

1 At the point of decrease, sew through two up-beads in the previous row (**figure 1**).

2 In the next row, when you reach the two-bead space, pick up one bead (**figure 2**).

3 Continue working in regular peyote stitch.

INCREASING

1 At the point of increase, pick up two beads instead of one. Sew through the next bead (**figure 3**).

2 When you reach the two beads in the next row, sew through the first bead, pick up a bead, and sew through the second bead. This is sometimes referred to as "splitting the increase" (**figure 4**).

3 Continue working in regular peyote stitch.

notes Not all beads of any given type are shaped the same, and you can use that to your advantage when increasing and decreasing. For instance, when you add two beads for an increase, choose two narrow beads. In the next row when you split the increase, use another narrow bead. In the following row, go back to using standard size beads.

Likewise, when decreasing, pick up a wide bead when you are going over the point of decrease. In the following rows, you can use regular size beads.

ADVANCED TECHNIQUES

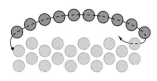

FIGURE 1

FIGURE 2

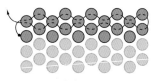

FIGURE 3

FAST PEYOTE

In fast peyote, you pick up all the beads for two rows or rounds at a time instead of repeatedly picking up one bead and stitching it in place. Be sure you are comfortable with the regular peyote technique before trying fast peyote so that you understand the mechanics of the stitch. This technique comes from Dona Anderson, who got it from a Native American friend.

FLAT EVEN-COUNT

1 Pick up an even number of beads to form rows 1 and 2. Work in flat even-count peyote stitch until you have a total of four rows.

2 Pick up the same number of beads you started with in step 1 (that is, enough beads for two rows). Drape them across the beadwork, and sew through the end up-bead in the previous row, going in the opposite direction (**figure 1**).

3 Skip the last bead picked up in step 2, sew through the next one, and continue through the next up-bead in the previous row (**figure 2, a–b**). Repeat this stitch across the row, zigzagging through every other bead picked up in step 2 and the up-beads in the previous row (**b–c**).

4 Repeat steps 2 and 3 for the desired length (**figure 3**).

FLAT ODD-COUNT

1 Pick up an odd number of beads to form rows 1 and 2. Work in flat odd-count peyote stitch until you have a total of four rows.

2 Exiting an edge down-bead, pick up the same number of beads you picked up to begin step 1. Drape them across the beadwork, and sew under the thread bridge on the opposite edge (**figure 1, a–b**). Sew through the last bead picked up, going in the opposite direction (**b–c**).

3 Sew through the next up-bead in the previous row, skip the next bead in the group you picked up in step 2, and sew through the following bead (**figure 2, a–b**). Repeat this stitch across the row, zigzagging through every other bead in the new group and the up-beads in the previous row. Exit the first bead picked up in step 2 (**b–c**).

4 Repeat steps 2 and 3 for the desired length.

note While fast peyote does hasten your stitching, you'll get bogged down if you pick up the wrong beads, so always double-check that you've got the right beads on your needle before stitching them in place.

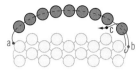

FIGURE 1

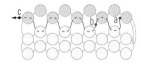

FIGURE 2

TUBULAR EVEN-COUNT

1 Pick up an even number of beads, tie them into a ring with a square knot, and sew through the first bead again.

2 Work in tubular even-count peyote stitch until you have a total of four rounds.

3 Pick up the same number of beads you picked up in step 1, and sew through the first bead just picked up (**photo a**).

4 Sew through the next up-bead in the previous round (**photo b**), skip the next bead in the group you picked up in step 3, and sew through the following bead (**photo c**). Repeat this stitch to complete the round, and step up through the first two beads picked up in this round (**photo d**).

5 Repeat steps 3 and 4 for the desired length.

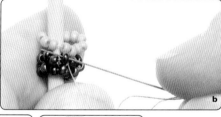

TUBULAR ODD-COUNT

1 Pick up an odd number of beads, tie them into a ring with a square knot, and sew through the first bead again.

2 Work in tubular odd-count peyote stitch until you have a total of four rounds.

3 Pick up the same number of beads you picked up in step 1, and sew through the first bead again.

4 Sew through the next up-bead in the previous round, skip the next bead in the group you picked up in step 3, and sew through the following bead. Repeat this stitch until you've sewn through the last bead picked up in step 3. You do not need to step up.

5 Repeat steps 3 and 4 for the desired length.

TIP For straight and precise lines and edges, be sure to cull your beads as you work, setting aside any that are too wide, narrow, or misshapen.

STITCH IN THE DITCH

The "stitch in the ditch" technique is done on top of an existing layer of peyote. Exit the beadwork as directed in the project instructions. Pick up a bead, and sew through the next bead in the same row. Repeat across the row or as directed.

PEYOTE TOGGLE CLASP

The following instructions make a ¾-in. (1.9 cm) toggle clasp. Adjust bead counts if you want a larger clasp.

To make a toggle ring: On 1 yd. (.9 m) of thread, pick up 36–40 15º seed beads, and tie them into a ring with a square knot, leaving a 12-in. (30 cm) tail. Work a round of even-count tubular peyote stitch using 15ºs, and then work two rounds with 11º seed beads or cylinder beads. Using the tail, work a round using 11ºs, and then zip up the two edge rounds to form a ring.

To make a toggle bar: On 1 yd. (.9 m) of thread, pick up 14–16 11º or 15º seed beads, leaving a 6-in. (15 cm) tail. Work a total of 10–14 rows of flat even- or odd-count peyote, roll the strip into a tube, and zip up the end rows.

note When your thread gets short, always add a new thread before ending the old one. Work a few rows or rounds with the new thread, and then end the old thread in the beadwork. This will ensure that you resume stitching in the right direction.

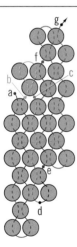

DIAGONAL PEYOTE

Diagonal peyote is a result of working flat peyote with an increase at one edge and a decrease at the other edge with every pair of rows.

1 To create a diagonal band, work three rows of flat even-count peyote stitch (**figure, a–b**).

2 Work an increase: Pick up three beads, and sew back through the first bead just picked up (**b–c**). Working in the other direction, continue in peyote stitch, stopping short of the final stitch in the row (**c–d**).

3 Work a decrease: Pick up a bead, and sew back through the last up-bead in the previous row (**d–e**). Continue in peyote to complete the row (**e–f**).

4 Repeat steps 2 and 3 (**f–g**) to the desired length, always working an increase along one edge and a decrease along the other edge.

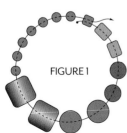

FIGURE 1

DUTCH SPIRAL

Similar to tubular Cellini spiral, Dutch spiral is a sculptural variant of tubular peyote. The distinguishing characteristic is a loose "bridge" of beads that spans one section of the beadwork, and it tends to be more flexible than tubular Cellini spiral. Just about any types of seed beads can be used in Dutch spiral. The beads used in the sample shown here are:

As – 11º hex-cut beads   **Ds** – 5º triangle beads
Bs – 10º seed beads   **Es** – 6º seed beads
Cs – 8º seed beads   **Fs** – 11º seed beads

1 Pick up an A, two Bs, two Cs, two Ds, two Es, and seven Fs. Tie the beads into a ring with a square knot, and sew through the A again (**figure 1**).

2 Work a round of tubular peyote, picking up the following beads, one per stitch: A, B, C, D (**figure 2, a–b**). Pick up an E and seven Fs, and sew through the A picked up at the start of the round (**b–c**).

3 Repeat step 2 for the desired length. Alternatively, you can vary the number of Fs picked up to create a piece with a graduated spiral.

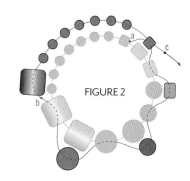

FIGURE 2

CELLINI SPIRAL

The Cellini spiral was originated by seed bead masters Virginia Blakelock and Carol Perrenoud, who developed the tubular variation and named it after Benvenuto Cellini, a 16th-century Italian sculptor known for his Rococo architectural columns. Eventually, the flat version emerged, and both techniques are equally beautiful.

FLAT CELLINI SPIRAL

1 Pick up two color A 15º seed beads, two color B 15º seed beads, two As, two color C 11º cylinder beads, and two color D 11º seed beads (**figure, a–b**). These beads will shift to form rows 1 and 2 as row 3 is added.

2 Work in flat even-count peyote stitch, picking up the following beads, one per stitch:

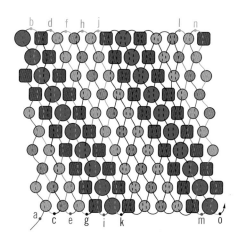

Row 3: C, D, C, A, B (**b–c**).
Row 4: B, A, C, D, C (**c–d**).
Row 5: A, C, D, C, A (**d–e**).
Row 6: A, C, D, C, A (**e–f**).
Row 7: B, A, C, D, C (**f–g**).
Row 8: C, D, C, A, B (**g–h**).
Row 9: A, B, A, C, D (**h–i**).
Row 10: D, C, A, B, A (**i–j**).
Row 11: C, A, B, A, C (**j–k**).

3 Rows 12–20: Work rows 11–3 in reverse (**k–l**).

4 Work three more rows to complete the pattern:
Row 21: A, B, A, C, D (**l–m**).
Row 22: D, C, A, B, A (**m–n**).
Row 23: C, A, B, A, C (**n–o**).

5 Repeat steps 3 and 4 until you reach the desired length.

TUBULAR CELLINI SPIRAL

1 Pick up two color A 15º seed beads, two color B 15º seed beads, two color C 11º cylinder beads, two color D 11º seed beads, two color E 8º seed beads, two Ds, and two Cs. Tie the beads into a ring with a square knot, and sew through the first two As again (**figure 1, a–b**). These beads will shift to form rounds 1 and 2 as round 3 is added.

2 Work round 3 in tubular peyote stitch, picking up the following beads, one per stitch: A, B, C, D, E, D, C. Step up through the first A in the new round (**b–c**).

3 Repeat step 2 (**figure 2**) to the desired length.

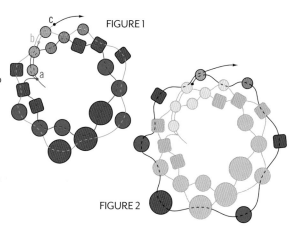

FIGURE 1

FIGURE 2

note To enhance the sculptural aspect of tubular Cellini spiral, gently squeeze the opening of the beadwork as you stitch. This will help you maintain the tension and prevent gaps between beads of different sizes.

PEYOTE BEZELS

If you want to capture round or shaped stones in beaded bezels, look no further. These instructions will show you how to make perfect peyote stitch bezels every time.

MATERIALS

each bezel crystal rivoli or shaped stone

- **1–2 g** 11° cylinder beads
- **1 g** 15° seed beads
- Fireline, 6 lb. test, or nylon beading thread, size D
- beading needles, #12

ROUND BEZELS

1 On 1 yd. (.9 m) of thread, pick up enough 11° cylinder beads to fit around the circumference of a rivoli or stone. See page 33 for the approximate number of cylinders to start with. Center the beads on the thread, and sew through the first cylinder again to form a ring **(figure 1, a–b)**.

2 Pick up a cylinder, skip the next cylinder in the ring, and sew through the following cylinder **(b–c)**. Continue working in tubular peyote stitch to complete the round, and step up through the first cylinder added **(c–d)**.

3 Work the next two rounds in tubular peyote using 15° seed beads **(d–e)**. Keep the tension tight to decrease the size of the ring.

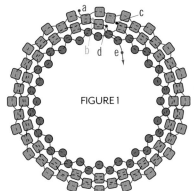

FIGURE 1

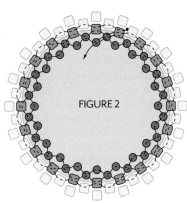

FIGURE 2

4 Position the rivoli or stone in the bezel cup. Using the other thread, work one round of tubular peyote along the other edge using cylinder beads, and two rounds using 15°s **(figure 2)**.

SQUARE RIVOLI (12 MM)

1 On a comfortable length of thread, pick up a repeating pattern of five cylinders and four 15°s four times, and sew through the first cylinder again **(figure 1, a–b)**, leaving a 12-in. (30 cm) tail.

2 Work two stitches in tubular peyote using cylinders **(b–c)**. Pick up a 15°, skip the first 15° in the ring, and sew through the next two 15°s **(c–d)**. Work one stitch with a 15° **(d–e)**. Repeat these stitches three times to complete the round, and step up to start the next round **(e–f)**.

3 Work a round of tubular peyote, picking up one 15° in each stitch, and treating the two 15°s at each corner as one bead **(f–g)**.

4 Work a peyote stitch, and sew through the next two 15°s without picking up a new 15° **(g–h)**. Pick up a 15°, and sew through the next up-15°. Continue around, decreasing at the remaining corners the same way **(h–i)**.

5 Place the rivoli in the bezel, and, using the tail thread, sew through the next 15° in the first round **(figure 2, a–b)**.

6 Pick up two 15°s, skip two 15°s, and sew through the next 15°. Work three peyote stitches using cylinders **(b–c)**. Repeat around, and step up **(c–d)**.

7 Work a round of tubular peyote using 15°s, sewing through the two 15°s at each corner as if they were a single bead, and step up **(d–e)**. Work a second round of 15°s to complete the bezel, treating the two-bead stitches as a single bead **(e–f)**.

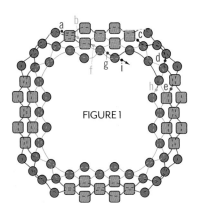

FIGURE 1

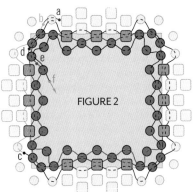

FIGURE 2

NAVETTE STONE (32 X 17 MM)

1 On a comfortable length of thread, pick up 29 cylinders and three 15⁰s twice, and sew through the first cylinder again to form a ring, leaving an 18-in. (46 cm) tail (**figure, a–b**).

2 Work a round of tubular peyote, picking up cylinders where you skip cylinders and 15⁰s where you skip 15⁰s (**b–c**).

3 Work a round of peyote picking up a 15⁰ for each stitch (**c–d**).

4 Work a round of peyote, picking up one 15⁰ for each stitch on the long sides (where the cylinders sit). Skip the center bead in each corner, picking up two 15⁰s to span the distance, instead of one (**d–e**).

5 Place the stone in the bezel so the back is nestled in the beads. If the hold is not secure, you may want to add two 15⁰s to each corner.

6 Using the tail thread, sew through the next 15⁰ (**a–aa**), and work a round of peyote, picking up a 15⁰ in each stitch. Sew through three 15⁰s to step up (**aa–bb**).

7 Work the final round as you did in step 4 (**bb–cc**).

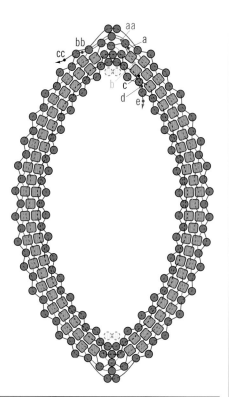

How many cylinders?

It can be challenging to guess how many cylinders to pick up in the initial bezel ring. Two important tips: The initial ring should always have an even number of beads, and it should fit around the widest part of your stone. Though these counts may vary slightly depending upon your beads and stitching tension, this is a good place to start when bezeling.

TRIANGULAR STONE (23 MM)

1 On a comfortable length of thread, pick up a repeating pattern of 17 cylinders and five 15⁰s three times, leaving an 18-in. (46 cm) tail. Sew through the first two cylinders again to form a ring (**figure, a–b**).

2 Work seven peyote stitches using cylinders (**b–c**), pick up a 15⁰, and sew through the next two 15⁰s (**c–d**). Pick up a 15⁰, skip the next 15⁰ in the ring, and sew through the next two 15⁰s (**d–e**). Pick up a 15⁰ skip the next cylinder, and sew through the following cylinder (**e–f**). Repeat around, and step up (**f–g**).

3 Work a round of tubular peyote, picking up one 15⁰ for each stitch (**g–h**).

4 Work seven peyote stitches, picking up one 15⁰ in each stitch, and then sew through the next 15⁰ without adding a bead (**h–i**). Continue around in tubular peyote, decreasing at each corner (**i–j**).

5 Fit the stone in the bezel, and, using the tail thread, pick up two 15⁰s, sew through the next 15⁰, pick up two 15⁰s, skip two 15⁰s, and sew through the next up-cylinder (**a–aa**). Work eight peyote stitches using cylinders (**aa–bb**). Repeat around the stone, then step up (**bb–cc**).

6 Work a round of peyote using the same stitch pattern as in step 2: a 15⁰, a 15⁰, seven cylinders, a 15⁰. Repeat around, and step up (**cc–dd**).

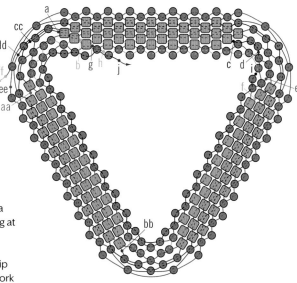

7 Work a round of tubular peyote, picking up one 15⁰ in each stitch, and step up (**dd–ee**).

8 Work a round of tubular peyote using 15⁰s and decreasing in each corner, as in step 4 (**ee–ff**).

NETTING BASICS

Gather some seed beads, your favorite needle and thread, and learn vertical, horizontal, tubular, and circular netting.

MATERIALS

samples

- **1–2 g** 11º seed beads
- Fireline, 6 lb. test, or nylon beading thread, size D
- beading needles, #11

TECHNIQUES

- beading fundamentals: attaching a stop bead, conditioning thread, ending and adding thread (p. 20)

HORIZONTAL AND VERTICAL NETTING

Horizontal and vertical netting have the same basic structure, and they are named for the orientation of how the stitches are worked. Both are commonly used to make simple bands, collar necklaces, or larger scarf-like sections of netted beadwork. The following instructions are for small sections of five-bead netting that introduce the basic technique, but netting can be worked with any number of beads per stitch. The more beads you use in each stitch, the larger the spaces between the stitches in the finished piece. Fewer beads produce a more fabric-like appearance. Work the following samples with comfortable lengths of thread. If desired, condition your thread.

note Netting is a close relative of peyote stitch; if you only picked up one bead per stitch, you would be working in peyote. Once you have made the samples, try varying the size of the netted stitches by altering the number of beads per stitch.

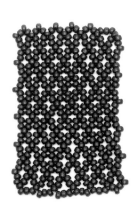

1 Pick up 40 11ºs seed beads, skip the last nine 11ºs, and sew through the next 11º, with your needle pointing toward the tail (**figure, a–b**).

2 Pick up five 11ºs, skip five 11ºs in the base row, and sew through the next 11º (**b–c**). Repeat to the row's end (**c–d**).

3 To turn and start the next row, pick up six 11ºs, skip three 11ºs in the previous row, and sew through the center 11º in the next stitch (**d–e**).

4 Repeat steps 2 and 3 to reach the desired length (**e–f**).

TUBULAR AND CIRCULAR NETTING

These two styles of netting have similar techniques also. Tubular netting creates a tube, and circular netting is flat, radiating from a center circle of beads.

TUBULAR NETTING

1 Pick up 24 11ºs, and sew through them again to create a ring, exiting the first 11º picked up.

2 Pick up five 11ºs, skip five 11ºs in the ring, and sew through the next 11º in the ring (**figure, a–b**). Repeat to complete the round (**b–c**). Step up through the first three 11ºs in the first stitch (**c–d**).

3 Pick up five 11ºs, skip five 11ºs in the previous round, and sew through the center 11º in the next stitch (**d–e**). Repeat to complete the round, and step up through three 11ºs in the first stitch (**e–f**).

4 Repeat step 3 to the desired length.

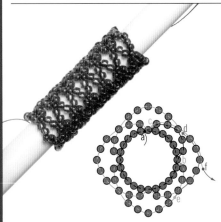

CIRCULAR NETTING

Each round of circular netting requires additional beads in each stitch to allow the piece to lie flat.

1 Pick up 10 11⁰s, sew through them again to create a ring, and exit the first 11⁰ picked up.
2 Pick up three 11⁰s, skip an 11⁰ in the ring, and sew through the next 11⁰ (**figure, a–b**). Repeat to complete the round, and step up through the first two 11⁰s in the first stitch (**b–c**).
3 Pick up five 11⁰s, skip three 11⁰s in the previous round, and sew through the center 11⁰ in the next stitch (**c–d**). Repeat to complete the round, and step up through the first three 11⁰s in the first stitch (**d–e**).
4 Continue adding rounds, increasing two beads per stitch per round to reach the desired size (**e–f**).

POINTS AND PICOTS

The technique described on the previous page results in rounded "loops" along each edge. For a more decorative edge, you can make points or picots.

POINTS

1 To create a point along the edges of the netted sample, pick up 38 11⁰s. Skip the last 11⁰, and sew through the next 11⁰ in the previous row with your needle pointing toward the tail (**figure 1, a–b**).
2 Pick up five 11⁰s, skip five 11⁰s in the previous row, and sew through the next 11⁰ (**b–c**). Repeat to complete the row (**c–d**).
3 To turn and start the next row, pick up four 11⁰s. Skip the last 11⁰, and sew through the next 11⁰ (**d–e**).
4 Repeat steps 2 and 3 to reach the desired length (**e–f**).

PICOTS

1 Pick up 40 11⁰s, skip the last three 11⁰s, and sew through the next 11⁰ in the previous row (**figure 2, a–b**).
2 Pick up five 11⁰s, and sew through the next 11⁰ in the previous row (**b–c**). Repeat to complete the row (**c–d**).
3 To turn and start the new row, pick up six 11⁰s, skip the last three 11⁰s, and sew through the next 11⁰ (**d–e**).
4 Repeat steps 2 and 3 to reach the desired length (**e–f**).

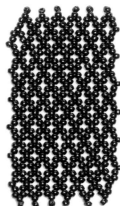

FIGURE 1

FIGURE 2

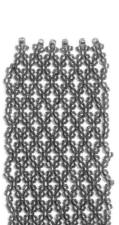

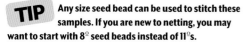

TIP Any size seed bead can be used to stitch these samples. If you are new to netting, you may want to start with 8⁰ seed beads instead of 11⁰s.

LADDER STITCH BASICS

The foundation stitch for other techniques, such as herringbone and brick stitch, the bead ladder proves itself useful time and time again.

MATERIALS

samples
- assorted triangle, cylinder, and/or bugle beads
- Fireline, 6 lb. test, or nylon beading thread, size D
- beading needles, #11

TECHNIQUES
- beading fundamentals: ending and adding thread (p. 20)

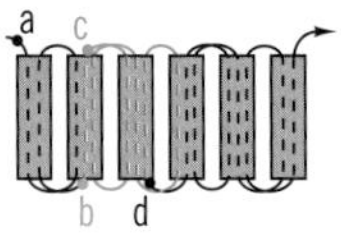

FIGURE 1

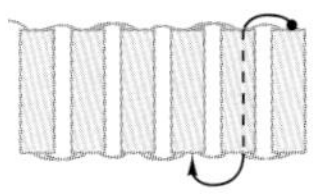

FIGURE 2

LADDER STITCH BASICS

As you work this stitch, the beads begin to resemble the rungs of a ladder — hence the name "ladder stitch." You can use almost any style of bead, or use two or more beads as one in each stitch, which results in a variety of looks that you can use in many ways. Ladder stitch is used most often as a base for brick stitch or herringbone stitch.

The traditional way to work ladder stitch is to pick up two beads and sew through the first bead (**figure 1, a–b**) and the second bead (**b–c**) again. Add subsequent beads by picking up one bead, sewing through the previous bead, and then sewing through the new bead (**c–d**).

This is the most common technique, but it produces uneven tension along the ladder of beads because of the alternating pattern of a single thread bridge on the edge between two beads and a double thread bridge on the opposite edge

between the same two beads. You can easily correct the uneven tension by zigzagging back through the beads in the opposite direction after you've stitched your ladder to the desired length (**figure 2**). Doing this creates a double thread path along both edges of the ladder.

This aligns the beads right next to each other but fills the bead holes with extra thread, which can cause a problem if you are using beads with small holes.

When you're using ladder stitch to create a base for brick stitch, having the holes filled with thread doesn't matter because the rows of brick stitch are worked off the thread bridges, not by sewing through the beads.

If you're using the ladder as a base for herringbone stitch, extra thread is potentially problematic, because you'll be sewing through the ladder base more than once.

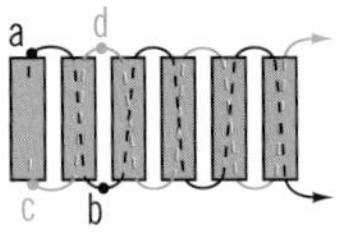

FIGURE 3

FIGURE 4

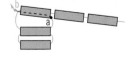

FIGURE 5

ALTERNATIVE LADDER STITCH METHODS

You may wish to try one of these two other ladder stitch methods, each of which produces beadwork with even tension. The first, a cross-needle technique, results in a single thread path on each edge. To begin, center a bead on the thread. Pick up a bead on one needle and cross the other needle through it (**figure 3, a–b and c–d**). Add each subsequent bead in the same manner.

To begin the other alternative method, pick up all the beads you need to reach the length your pattern requires. Fold the last two beads so they are parallel, and sew through the second-to-last bead in the same direction (**figure 4, a–b**). Fold the next loose bead so it sits parallel to the previous bead in the ladder, and sew through the loose bead in the same direction (**figure 5, a–b**). Continue sewing through each bead until you exit the last bead of the ladder.

CREATING A RING

If you are working in tubular brick stitch or herringbone stitch, sew your ladder into a ring to provide a base for the new technique.

With your thread exiting the last bead in your ladder, sew through the first bead and then through the last bead, or cross the needles through the first bead if you are using the two-needle technique.

TIP The ladder at the bottom has only one bead per stitch; the next has bugle beads; the next has triangle beads, the points of which nestle together; and the top sample has two beads per stitch.

TIP If you've had a hard time working odd-count peyote, try this stitch combination: Work a strip of flat even-count peyote to the desired length. Working off the beads along one edge of the strip as if it were a ladder stitch base, stitch a row of brick stitch to transform the strip into flat odd-count peyote.

BRICK STITCH

The offset rows of brick stitch resemble a brick wall.

The exact origin of brick stitch is unknown, as is the date of its creation. Early examples of brick stitch have been found in the handiwork of native beaders in Africa and North America. One characteristic of the stitch is that you attach each bead to the thread bridge of a previous row rather than by sewing through other beads. This allows for a great deal of flexibility in combining beads of varying sizes and shapes.

MATERIALS

samples
- 8⁰ or 11⁰ seed beads
- Fireline, 6 lb. test, or nylon beading thread, size D
- beading needles, #11

TECHNIQUES
- ladder stitch (p. 36)

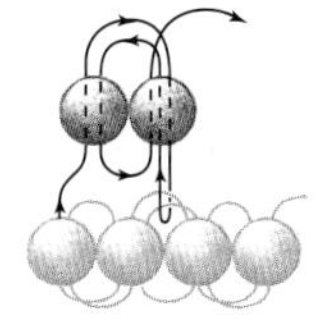

FLAT BRICK STITCH

FIGURE 1

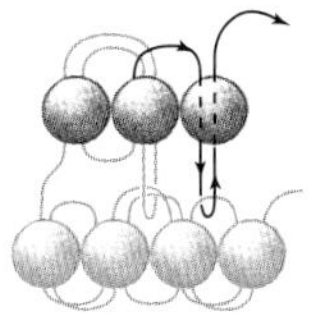

FIGURE 2

Begin with a ladder of beads, and position the thread to exit the top of the last bead. Brick stitch naturally increases or decreases at the start and end of each row, depending upon where you attach the first and last stitches of the row. To work the typical method, which results in progressively decreasing rows, pick up two beads. Sew under the thread bridge between the second and third beads in the previous row from back to front. Sew up through the second bead added, down through the first bead, and back up through the second bead (**figure 1**).

For the row's remaining stitches, pick up one bead. Sew under the next thread bridge in the previous row from back to front. Sew back up through the new bead. The last stitch in the row will be positioned above the last two beads in the row below, and the row will be one bead shorter than the ladder (**figure 2**).

BRICK STITCH INCREASE

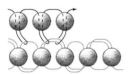

FIGURE 3

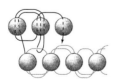

FIGURE 4

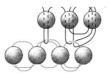

FIGURE 5

A single increase in the row will keep the number of beads the same as in the previous row. To increase at the beginning of a row, work a typical brick stitch, but start by sewing under the thread bridge between the first two beads in the previous row (**figure 3**).

To increase within a row, add a second stitch to the same thread bridge as the previous stitch. To increase at the end of the row, add a second stitch to the final thread bridge on the previous row (**figures 4 and 5**).

BRICK STITCH DECREASE

Brick stitch naturally decreases by one bead in each row. To decrease by more than one bead within a row, skip a thread bridge, and complete the stitch **(figure 6)**.

To create a larger-than-normal decrease at the end of a row, stop short of the last bead in the previous row **(figure 7)**.

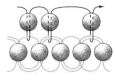

FIGURE 6

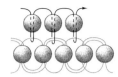

FIGURE 7

CIRCULAR BRICK STITCH

You can work in a circular pattern to create a round of brick-stitched beads.

CONTINUOUS SPIRAL

Begin with a ladder of beads, and position the thread to exit the bottom of the second-to-last bead. Overlap the first two beads in the ladder with the last two beads. Sew down through the first bead and up through the second bead. Sew up through the last bead. Once this join is complete, you can work brick stitch continuously around the ring to form a tube or rope **(figure 8)**.

FIGURE 8

LEVEL ROWS

Begin with a ladder of beads, and join the two ends. Position the thread to exit the top of a bead **(figure 9)**. Following the instructions for flat brick stitch, pick up two beads to begin the row **(figure 10)**. Continue around the ring. Join the last and first beads by stitching down through the first bead and back up through the last bead **(figure 11)**. Continue working one round at a time, stepping up to begin each new round.

FIGURE 9

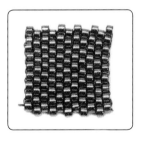

FIGURE 10

FIGURE 11

SQUARE STITCH

Learn this straightforward stitch for sturdy beadwork.

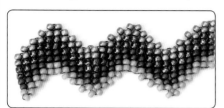

Beadwork stitched in square stitch looks like a grid: The beads are stacked directly above and below each other in parallel rows. Square stitch resembles loomwork, and patterns for the two techniques are often interchangeable. Square stitch is especially useful for small pieces for which a loom isn't practical — pieces that use beads in multiple sizes, and those with increases and decreases along the edges. It is also sturdy, which is desirable if you are making jewelry that will get a lot of wear.

MATERIALS

samples

- **1–2 g** 8° or 11° seed beads
- Fireline, 6 lb. test, or nylon beading thread, size D
- beading needles, #11

TECHNIQUES

- beading fundamentals: attaching a stop bead, ending and adding thread (p. 20)

FIGURE 1

FIGURE 2

SQUARE STITCH BASICS

1 Pick up the required number of beads for the first row, then pick up the first bead of the next row. Sew through the last bead of the previous row and the first bead of the current row again (**figure 1**).

2 Pick up a bead, and sew through the next-to-last bead of the previous row and the bead just picked up (**figure 2**). Repeat across the row.

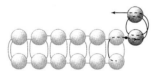

FIGURE 3

INCREASING

1 To increase the width of your work by one bead, pick up two beads at the end of a row. Sew through them both again (**figure 3**), then resume working across the established row.

2 To make a matching increase on the other edge, complete the row, then pick up two beads. Sew through them again, then sew through the end bead in the previous row and the two end beads in the new row (**figure 4**).

FIGURE 4

DECREASING

To decrease the width of your work, sew through the beadwork to exit the bead below where the new bead will be added. Pick up a bead, and sew through the bead your thread just exited and the new bead (**figure 5**). Continue in square stitch across the row.

FIGURE 5

TWO-BEAD SQUARE STITCH

1 Pick up an even number of beads for the first row. Pick up two beads, and sew through the last two beads in the first row and the new beads (**figure 6, a–b**).
2 Pick up two beads, and sew through the next two beads in the previous row and the new beads (**b–c**). Repeat across the row.

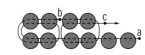

FIGURE 6

HERRINGBONE STITCH

Herringbone stitch (also called Ndebele) has been used by beaders of the Ndebele tribe in southern Africa for centuries. Its distinctive weave places pairs of beads side-by-side in slightly angled stacks, creating a zigzag effect across the horizontal rows and a ribbed effect in the vertical stacks. In this tutorial, you will learn three approaches to the stitch.

The stitch can either start from a row of beads that is gathered into stacks as the second row is sewn, or from a row of ladder-stitched beads. The traditional way to begin the stitch allows the beads in the base row to angle slightly, following the overall pattern of the weave. When working from a ladder base, the first row will be straight. The angled bead pairs begin in the second row.

MATERIALS

samples

- **1–2 g** 8º or 11º seed beads in each of 2 colors: A, B
- Fireline, 6 lb. test, or nylon beading thread, size D
- beading needles, #11

TECHNIQUES

- beading fundamentals: attaching a stop bead, ending and adding thread (p. 20)
- ladder stitch (p. 36)

FIGURE 1

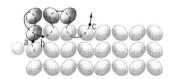

FIGURE 2

FLAT HERRINGBONE

TRADITIONAL START

1 On a comfortable length of thread, attach a stop bead, leaving a tail equal to the desired width of the band plus 6 in. (15 cm). Pick up an even number of beads in multiples of four. Allow a small amount of space between the beads and the stop bead. These beads will form the first two rows.
2 Pick up a bead, and sew back through the end bead. Skip two beads, and sew up through the next bead (**figure 1, a–b**).
3 Pick up two beads, and sew down through the next bead. Skip two beads, and sew up through the next bead (**b–c**). Repeat across the row.
4 To finish the row and begin the next: with your thread exiting the end bead, pick up two beads, and sew down through the first bead just picked up (**figure 2, a–b**).
5 Sew up through the next bead, and pick up two beads. Sew down through the following bead, and continue up through the subsequent bead (**b–c**). Repeat the last stitch to continue adding pairs of beads across the row. Begin to snug up the stacks.
6 When you have completed the beadwork, remove the stop bead. Use the tail to sew across the first row to connect the stacks.

This method will create a half-stack along the edge with thread showing on every-other bead (**photo a**). If you want to avoid having exposed thread, pick up two beads at the first turn and three beads at all other turns. Sew into the first bead just picked up. This will position a bead at the edge of every other row (**photo b, left edge**). You may choose to fill in the gaps between the edge beads to create the effect of a stack on each edge (**right edge**).

a

b

FLAT HERRINGBONE
LADDER START: EVEN-COUNT

1 Using an even-count row will stack pairs of beads across the beadwork. Start with an even number of beads stitched into a ladder. Turn the ladder, if necessary, so your thread exits the end bead pointing up.

2 Pick up two beads, and sew down through the next bead in the ladder (**figure 3, a–b**). Sew up through the third bead in the ladder, pick up two beads, and sew down through the fourth bead (**b–c**). Repeat across the ladder.

3 To make the turn, sew down through the end bead of the previous row and back through the last bead of the pair you just added (**figure 4, a–b**). Pick up two beads, sew down through the next bead in the previous row, and sew up through the following bead (**b–c**). Continue adding pairs of beads across the row. You may choose to hide the edge thread by picking up an accent or smaller bead before you sew back through the last bead of the pair you just added.

More possibilities: To make a turn without having thread show on an edge or adding an edge bead, sew down through the end bead of the previous row, up through the second-to-last bead in the previous row, and continue through the last bead added (**figure 5, a–b**). Pick up two beads, sew down through the next bead in the previous row, and sew up through the following bead (**b–c**). Continue adding pairs of beads across the row. Using this turn will flatten the angle of the edge bead, making the edge stack look a little different than the others.

FIGURE 3

FIGURE 4

FIGURE 5

FLAT HERRINGBONE
LADDER START: ODD-COUNT

1 Using an odd-count row will create a half-stack of beads on one edge. Start with an odd number of beads stitched into a ladder. Turn the ladder, if necessary, so your thread exits the end bead pointing up.

2 Pick up two beads, and sew down through the next bead in the ladder. Sew up through the third bead in the ladder, pick up two beads, and sew down through the fourth bead. Repeat across the ladder.

3 To make the turn, sew up through the last bead in the row. Pick up two beads, and sew down through the first bead just picked up (**figure 6, a–b**). Sew up through the next bead on the previous row (**b–c**). Continue adding pairs of beads across the row. Make the turn on the other edge the same way as the turn for the even-count ladder version.

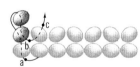

FIGURE 6

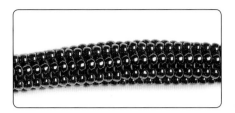

TUBULAR HERRINGBONE

Tubular herringbone usually starts from a ladder of beads formed into a ring, though it can also begin with a simple ring of beads. In either case, begin with an even number of beads. Once you get started, you can choose to make the ribs of the stitch straight (top) or twisted (bottom).

STRAIGHT TUBULAR HERRINGBONE

For a ladder start, stitch a ladder with an even number of beads, and form it into a ring. Your thread should exit the top of a bead. Pick up two beads, and sew down through the next bead in the previous round (**figure 7, a–b**). Sew up through the next bead, and repeat around the ring to complete the round (**b–c**). Step up to start the next round: Sew up through two beads — the next bead in the previous round and the first bead added in the new round (**c–d**).

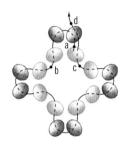

FIGURE 7

Alternatively, begin by picking up four beads, and sew through them again to form a ring. Sew through the first bead again, and snug up the beads (**figure 8, a–b**). Pick up two beads and sew through the next bead (**b–c**). Repeat three times, and step up through the first bead picked up in this round (**c–d**).

FIGURE 8

Whether you began with a ladder or a ring, continue adding two beads per stitch. As you work, snug up the beads to form a tube, and step up at the end of each round until your rope is the desired length.

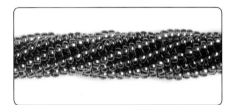

TWISTED TUBULAR HERRINGBONE

Form a base ring with an even number of beads. Pick up two beads, and sew through the next bead in the previous round (**figure 9, a–b**). Sew up through the next bead, and repeat around the ring to complete the round (**b–c**). Step up to start the next round by sewing up through two beads — the next bead in the previous round and the first bead added in the new round (**c–d**). Work one round of straight herringbone (**d–e**).

To create a twist in the tube, pick up two beads, sew down through one bead in the next stack and up through two beads in the following stack (**e–f**). Repeat around the ring, adding two beads per stitch. Step up to the next round through three beads (**f–g**). Snug up the beads to form a tube. The twist will begin to appear after the sixth round. Continue until your rope is the desired length.

To create a twist in the other direction, work the first two rounds as described. Pick up two beads, sew down through two beads in the next stack and up through one bead in the following stack. Repeat around the ring, adding two beads per stitch. Step up to the next round through two beads.

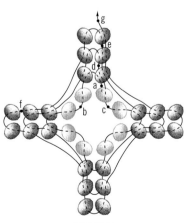

FIGURE 9

INCREASING IN TUBULAR HERRINGBONE

Increases are usually made between stitches. In the first increase round, pick up a single bead between the stitches (**figure 10, a–b**). You will not stitch through these single beads; they are used to fill in the space between rounds. In the next round, pick up two beads between the pairs of beads (**b–c**). In subsequent rounds, work in tubular herringbone with the increase pairs as bases for new stacks of beads (**c–d**). The increase stacks may initially seem shorter than the other stacks, but they will catch up as you work additional rounds.

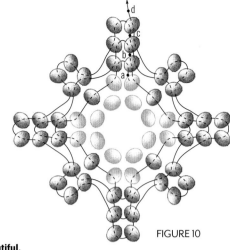

FIGURE 10

 TIP Straight or twisted, both tubular herringbone options are beautiful.

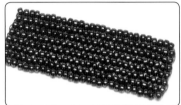

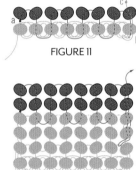

FIGURE 11

FIGURE 12

FIGURE 13

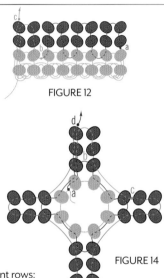

FIGURE 14

FASTER HERRINGBONE

Learn a faster way to work this popular stitch. Once you get the hang of regular herringbone stitch, work two rows at once to speed your progress.

FLAT ACCELERATED HERRINGBONE

1 On a comfortable length of thread, make a ladder of eight 11º seed beads, leaving a 6-in. (15 cm) tail. Zigzag back through the ladder so the working thread and tail are exiting opposite ends of the first bead.
2 Work a row of regular flat herringbone stitch using 11ºs (**figure 11, a–b**). To step up at the end of the row, sew under the bottom thread bridge between the last two beads in the ladder, and sew back through the next two edge 11ºs (**b–c**).
3 Work a row of accelerated herringbone: Pick up four 11ºs per stitch instead of two, stopping short of the last stitch (**figure 12, a–b**).
4 To work the last stitch and step up at the end of an accelerated row, sew up through the next 11º in the previous row. Pick up four 11ºs, sew down through two beads instead of one, sew under the bottom thread bridge between the first two beads in the ladder, and sew back through the next

four edge 11ºs (**b–c**).
5 To work subsequent rows: Continue adding rows as in steps 3 and 4, but in step 4 sew under the thread bridge between the last two beads in the previous row instead of the bottom thread bridge of the ladder (**figure 13**). Add rows to reach the desired length.

TUBULAR ACCELERATED HERRINGBONE

1 On a comfortable length of thread, pick up eight 11ºs, leaving a 6-in. (15 cm) tail. Tie the beads into a ring with a square knot, leaving a little space between the beads. Sew through the first 11º in the ring.
2 Pick up two 11ºs, and sew through the next two 11ºs in the ring. Repeat around the ring, and step up through the first 11º added in this round (**figure 14, a–b**).
3 Work a round of accelerated tubular herringbone: Pick up four 11ºs, sew down through the next 11º, and sew up through the following 11º in the previous round (**b–c**). Repeat to complete the round, and step up through the first two 11ºs picked up in the first stitch of this round (**c–d**). Continue adding rounds to reach the desired length.

45

RIGHT-ANGLE WEAVE

Right-angle weave is an off-loom beadweaving technique in which the beads of each stitch form a small square. You can use more than one bead on each side of the square, but in the following instructions, we'll show just one.

Beadwork made in right-angle weave, or its two-needle cousin — which is often called crossweave or two-needle weave — is evident in several cultures. Some of the beadwork dates as far back as the 1600s. David Chatt's development and expansion of single-needle techniques is largely responsible for the widespread interest in and use of right-angle weave today. In this section, you'll discover three variations of right-angle weave — flat, tubular, and cubic.

MATERIALS

samples
· **1–2 g** 11º seed beads in 2 colors
· Fireline, 6 lb. test, or nylon beading thread, size D
· beading needles, #11

TECHNIQUES
· beading fundamentals: square knot, ending and adding thread (p. 20)

RIGHT-ANGLE WEAVE

1 To start the first row of right-angle weave, pick up four beads, and tie them into a ring. Sew through the first beads again **(figure 1)**.

2 Pick up three beads. Sew through the bead your thread just exited **(figure 2, a–b)**, and continue through the first two beads picked up in this stitch **(b–c)**.

3 Continue adding three beads per stitch until the first row is the desired length. You are sewing rings in a figure 8 pattern, alternating direction with each stitch **(figure 3)**.

4 To begin row 2, sew through the last three beads of the last stitch in row 1, exiting the end bead at the edge of one long side **(figure 4)**.

5 Pick up three beads, and sew through the bead your thread exited in the previous step **(figure 5, a–b)**. Continue through the first new bead **(b–c)**.

6 Pick up two beads, and sew through the next top bead in the previous row and the bead your thread exited in the previous stitch **(figure 6, a–b)**. Continue through the two new beads and the next top bead of the previous row **(b–c)**.

7 Pick up two beads, and sew through the last two beads your thread went through in the previous stitch and the first new bead. Keep the thread moving in a figure 8. Pick up two beads per stitch for the rest of the row **(figure 7)**.

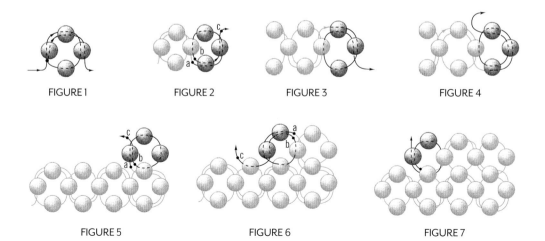

FIGURE 1   FIGURE 2   FIGURE 3   FIGURE 4

FIGURE 5   FIGURE 6   FIGURE 7

TUBULAR RIGHT-ANGLE WEAVE

1 Work a flat strip of right-angle weave that is one stitch fewer than needed for the desired circumference of the tube.
2 Connect the last stitch to the first stitch as follows: Exit the end bead of the last stitch, pick up one bead, sew through the first bead of the first stitch, and pick up one bead **(figure 8)**. Complete the connecting stitch by retracing the thread path. Exit as shown in the figure.
3 In subsequent rounds, you'll add three beads in the first stitch, two beads in the next stitches, and only one bead in the final stitch.

FIGURE 8

CUBIC RIGHT-ANGLE WEAVE

Cubic or three-dimensional right-angle weave moves your beadwork from a flat surface into more exciting forms and infinite possibilities. Cubic right-angle weave can be stitched two ways. You can work a string of cubes, or you can create one or more layers on top of a flat right-angle weave surface. The string of cubes could be a necklace, while the layered squares of right angle-weave could be, among other things, the start of a small box.

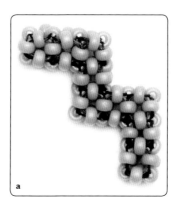

a

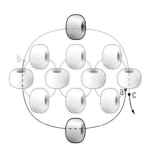

FIGURE 1

STRING OF CUBES

Each cube is like a box with six surfaces — four sides, a top, and a bottom. Each side is made up of four beads, but since the beads are shared, only 12 beads are used to make the first cube, and eight beads are used for each cube thereafter. The cubes can be stacked on top of each other or worked off of different sides to make zigzags **(photo a)**.
1 To begin, work three right-angle weave stitches. Bring the ends together, and connect them: Pick up a bead, sew through the opposite end bead **(figure 1, a–b)**, pick up a bead, and sew through the other end bead **(b–c)**. Figure 2 shows a three-dimensional view of the resulting cube. To make the cube more stable, sew through all four beads on the top of the cube **(figure 3)**. Sew through the beadwork to the bottom of the cube, and sew through the four beads on that side to snug them up.

FIGURE 2

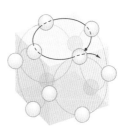

FIGURE 3

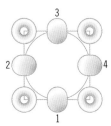

FIGURE 4

FIGURE 5

FIGURE 6

FIGURE 7

FIGURE 8

2 To make the next cube, work a right-angle weave stitch off of each of the top beads in the existing cube **(figure 4)**. For the first stitch, pick up three beads, and sew through the same top bead and the first bead just picked up **(figure 5)**. For the next stitch, pick up two beads, sew through the next top bead, the bead your thread exited at the start of this stitch, and the two beads just picked up **(figure 6)**. For the third stitch, sew through the next top bead, and pick up two beads. Sew through the side bead in the previous stitch, the third top bead, and the first bead just picked up **(figure 7)**. For the fourth stitch, pick up one bead, and sew down through the side bead in the first stitch, the fourth top bead, the side bead in the previous stitch, and the bead just picked up **(figure 8)**.

3 As you complete the cube, make sure you sew through the four new top beads to stabilize the structure. Continue for the desired length.

LAYERS OF CUBES

Adding a second layer to a flat surface is done by stitching perpendicular rows parallel to each other on a base of right-angle weave, and then connecting them at the top.

1 To begin, make a flat square of right-angle weave five stitches wide and tall, alternating dark and light rows. By alternating the colors of the rows, you'll be able to see the pattern more clearly. It will also help you see where to make the stitches.

2 Hold the base so the first dark row (the widest strip) is positioned vertically on the right **(figure 9)**. The beads you'll stitch through have the holes oriented from top to bottom. The rows are numbered in the working sequence.

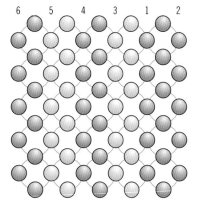

FIGURE 9

3 Sew down through the first bead in row 1. Pick up three dark beads, and sew through the base bead again, making a loop **(photo b)**.

4 Sew up through one bead, pick up two dark beads, and sew through the next base bead in row 1 and the end bead in the previous stitch.

5 Sew through the two new beads and the next base bead, pick up two dark beads, and sew through the end bead in the previous stitch and the next base bead in row 1.

6 Repeat steps 4 and 5 to the end of the row.

7 Using dark beads, work the second row of stitches off of the outside edge (row 2). This row will not stand perpendicular to the base yet — it will look just like any other row. When this row is complete, fold it up to create two parallel rows **(photo c)**.

8 Add one bead at a time to connect the two parallel rows: With your thread coming out of the bottom of the first right-row bead, pick up a dark bead, and sew up through the corresponding left-row bead **(figure 10, a–b)**.

9 Pick up a dark bead, and sew down through the right-row bead to complete the cubic unit. Continue through the lower dark bead you just added **(b–c)**.

10 Sew down through the next bead in the nearest parallel row, pick up a dark bead, sew up through the next bead in the opposite row, and continue around until you sew through the new bead again **(c–d)**.

11 Repeat step 10 to the end of the rows, adding six beads to bridge the parallel rows. After adding the last bead, sew around the edge beads to incorporate the base, and tighten the end before starting the next row **(photo d)**.

12 Work the third row using light beads, and then connect it to the previous dark row with light beads, as in steps 8–11. Continue to alternate the colors, connecting the previous row using the color of the row just worked.

13 Continue making layers to the desired length. Or, to make a hollow box from a cubic base, first work a perpendicular row one row in from the edges around the whole base **(photo e)**, then work a perpendicular row off the edge beads of the base **(photo f)**. Connect the two rows at the top to form a wall **(photo g)**. Continue this sequence to the desired height.

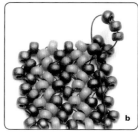
b

c

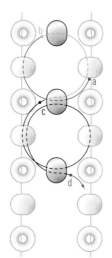

d

FIGURE 10

e

f

g

49

CROSSWEAVE TECHNIQUE

Just like it sounds, crossweave stitches are worked by crossing two thread paths through the same beads. You will need two needles to work this easy stitch. You can use the basics of crossweave technique to create a ladder (see "Ladder Stitch Basics," p. 36).

MATERIALS

samples
· bugle beads, seed beads, and other beads in various shapes
· Fireline, 6 lb. test, or nylon beading thread, size D
· **2** beading needles, #11

TECHNIQUES
· beading fundamentals: ending and adding thread (p. 20)

SINGLE BEAD

Thread a needle on each end of a piece of thread, and center a seed bead (or in these illustrations, a bugle bead). With the right-hand needle, pick up another bugle. Cross the left-hand needle through the bugle you just picked up. Repeat as desired.

MULTIPLE BEADS

1 Thread a needle on each end of a piece of thread, and center 16 seed beads. With the right-hand needle, cross through the last four seed beads to form a chain unit (**figure 1**). With the left-hand needle, pick up eight seed beads.
2 With the right-hand needle, pick up four seed beads, and cross through the last four seed beads picked up with the left-hand needle (**figure 2**).
3 Repeat step 2 to the desired length.
4 For the last unit, pick up eight seed beads with the left-hand needle, and pick up four seed beads with the right-hand needle. Tie the two threads together with a square knot to form the last chain unit, and end the threads.

You can use a combination of beads and bead types in various shapes and sizes to work in crossweave (**figure 3**).

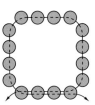

FIGURE 1

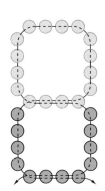

FIGURE 2

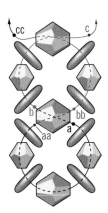

FIGURE 3

TIP You can use any even number of beads in crossweave technique.

FRINGE

Unfinished edges and visible thread can distract from the overall appeal of a design. A good way to tackle this problem is to learn about edging techniques. Embellish the edges of your work with any of these six types of fringe. There are a lot of different ways to embellish an edge, including short and long fringe, picot technique, a variation of beaded backstitch (adopted from bead embroidery), netting techniques, loops, and other decorative embellishments like leaves and petals.

These edging techniques are shown on a flat peyote base, but the orientation of the edge beads are the same in brick stitch, loomwork, and square stitch so you could modify these techniques to embellish the edges of these stitches as well.

MATERIALS

samples
- seed beads and larger beads as desired
- Fireline, 6 lb. test, or nylon beading thread, size D
- beading needles, #11

TECHNIQUES
- beading fundamentals: ending and adding thread (p. 20)

SHORT OR LONG FRINGE
Pick up at least two beads, skip the last bead picked up, and sew back through the rest of the beads. Sew through the next two edge beads (**figure 1, a–b**). You can make the fringe all the same length, alternate between two lengths, or graduate the lengths for an undulating effect. Fringe can be made with all the same type of bead or several different styles and sizes.

PICOT TECHNIQUE
Pick up four beads, skip the last three beads, sew back through the first bead picked up, and sew through the next two edge beads (**b–c**). Picot technique can also be used at the ends of fringe if desired (**c–d**).

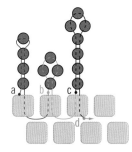

FIGURE 1

BEADED BACKSTITCH
Pick up three or four beads, lay them along the edge of the base, and sew through an adjacent edge bead. Sew through the previous edge bead, and then sew through the last one or two embellishment beads (**figure 2**).

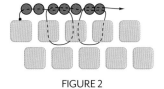

FIGURE 2

NETTING TECHNIQUES
Pick up three beads, and sew through the next two edge beads (**figure 3, a–b**). You can pick up any odd number of beads, but you may need to space out the netting by skipping one or more edge beads between stitches. You can also anchor the netted edging by picking up an odd number of beads for the first stitch, sewing through two edge beads, and then sewing back through the last bead in the previous netted stitch (**b–c**). For each subsequent stitch, pick up one less bead than the number picked up in the first stitch (**c–d**).

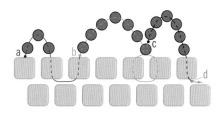

FIGURE 3

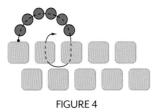

FIGURE 4

LOOPS

Pick up about five or six beads, skip the next edge bead, sew through the following edge bead, and sew through the skipped edge bead (**figure 4**). Repeat. The loops will overlap diagonally across the edge. If desired, you can pick up more beads in each stitch, creating larger loops, but you'll need to skip more edge beads.

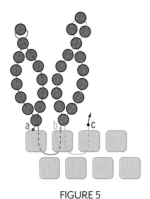

FIGURE 5

LEAVES OR PETALS

Pick up eight beads, skip the last bead picked up, and sew back through the next bead. Pick up five beads, sew through the first bead picked up, and continue through the next two edge beads (**figure 5, a–b**). The number of beads you pick up first will determine the size of your leaf or petal, and you'll always pick up three fewer beads than you did in the first half of the stitch to finish the second half. If desired, use the picot technique at the end of the leaf or petal (**b–c**).

TIP These are basic edging techniques. To make them really fit your design, incorporate beads used in the base along with complementary accent beads, or try a combination of these techniques to add flair to a flat band.

BEAD EMBROIDERY

Learn eight basic techniques for embellishing fabric or leather. Embellishing fabric or leather with beads is an ancient tradition in cultures around the world. In early days, beads were attached with thin strips of sinew, leather, or fiber in designs that identified them culturally or geographically. Their designs reflected patterns observed in nature and symbolic interpretations of their beliefs.

You can bead-embroider directly on the fabric or leather of your desired project or you can do your beading on a beading foundation, such as Lacy's Stiff Stuff, which provides stability and support for the beads and allows for easier stitching. To get started, thread a needle with a comfortable length of thread, and tie an overhand knot at the end. Sew up through the fabric or foundation at the point where you wish to begin beading. Work your design using the desired beads and stitches, ending your thread either on the back of the work or within the beadwork when your thread runs short.

For a nice finish, attach a backing layer of leather or Ultrasuede to hide the exposed stitching on the back, and then work an edging stitch around the perimeter to camouflage the seam.

MATERIALS

samples
· assorted beads
· fabric, leather, or beading foundation
· backing material, such as leather or Ultrasuede
· nylon beading thread, size D
· beading needles, #11 or #11 sharps

TECHNIQUES
· beading fundamentals: overhand knot, ending and adding thread (p. 20)

BEADED BACKSTITCH

On the top surface of the fabric or foundation, pick up three beads, snug them up, and align them as desired. Sew down through the fabric next to the last bead. Sew up through the fabric between the first and second beads, and sew through the second and third beads **(figure 1)**. Repeat for the desired length. To reinforce the stitching and to smooth the line, sew through the row of beads again without stitching through the fabric.

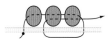

FIGURE 1

BUGLE BEAD STITCH

On the top surface of the fabric, pick up a seed bead, a bugle bead, and a seed bead, snug them up, and align them on top of the fabric. Sew down through the fabric next to the last seed bead and up through the fabric next to the first seed bead. Sew through the three beads again **(figure 2)**. In subsequent stitches, pick up a bugle and a seed bead, and sew through the last seed bead in the previous stitch and the two new beads. The seed beads prevent the sharp edges of the bugles from cutting the thread.

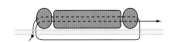

FIGURE 2

COUCHING

This stitch uses two separate needles and thread.
1 On the top surface of the fabric, pick up 10 to 12 beads with one needle, and align them on top of the fabric.
2 With the other needle, sew up through the fabric between the second and third beads. Pull the thread over the base thread between the beads, and sew down through the fabric on the other side of the thread. Repeat along the row of beads at two- or three-bead intervals to anchor the base thread to the fabric **(figure 3)**.
3 When the first section of beads is anchored, repeat steps 1 and 2.

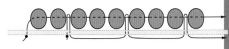

FIGURE 3

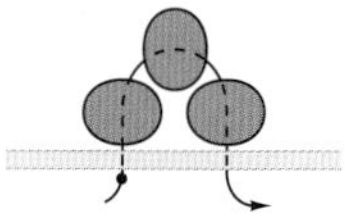

FIGURE 4

MOSS STITCH

On the top surface of the fabric, pick up three beads, and sew back through the fabric approximately one bead's width away (**figure 4**) to form a picot-like stitch.

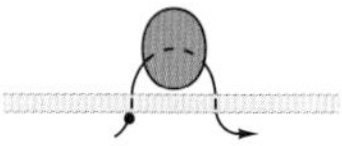

FIGURE 5

SEED STITCH

On the top surface of the fabric, pick up a bead, position it on the fabric, and sew back through the fabric next to the bead (**figure 5**).

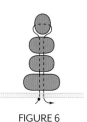

FIGURE 6

STACKS (SHORT FRINGE)

On the top surface of the fabric, pick up three or more beads, skip the last bead, and sew back through the other beads and the fabric (**figure 6**).

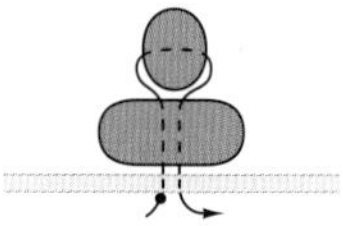

FIGURE 7

STOP STITCH

On the top surface of the fabric, pick up two beads, skip the last bead, and sew back through the first bead and the fabric (**figure 7**). The first bead is usually larger than the second bead.

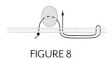

FIGURE 8

TRAVELING STITCH

The traveling stitch is useful in projects in which there is a hard surface, such as a button form, under the fabric because the needle passes through the fabric at an extreme angle, causing it to exit quite a distance from the last stitch.

To make a traveling stitch, sew up through the fabric after adding the previous bead. Without adding any beads, sew back through the fabric near the spot where the needle just exited, and sew up through the fabric again next to the previous stitch (**figure 8**).

SPIRALS & HELIXES

The spiral form, defined as a curve that turns around a central point or axis, can be found in many aspects of life, including nature, architecture, art, religion, and science. Beadwork is rich in spiral techniques, which can be confusing if you don't know how to tell them apart. In fact, any tubular stitch can feature a spiral pattern simply by using two or more colors positioned just so. However, there are particular stitches and variations that inherently produce spirals, and this workshop shows examples of some of these spiral stitches and how to achieve them. Here, you'll learn to identify and stitch three classic spirals.

MATERIALS

samples
- 11º and 8º seed beads (in multiple colors)
- assorted triangle, cylinder, and/or bugle beads
- assorted 3–4 mm accent beads, including pearls, bicone crystals, and glass beads
- Fireline, 6 lb. test, or nylon beading thread, size D
- beading needles, #11

TECHNIQUES
- beading fundamentals: ending and adding thread, square knot (p. 20)

SPIRAL ROPE

Spiral rope is a very easy stitch to learn. It features a core of beads with loops of additional beads that rotate around the core, creating the spiral pattern.

1 On a comfortable length of thread, pick up four color A and three color B 11º seed beads, and sew through the four As again (**figure 1**), leaving a 6-in. (15 cm) tail. The Bs will create a small loop. Move the loop to the left of the As.

2 Pick up an A and three Bs, and sew through the top three As from the previous stitch and the new A added in this stitch (**figure 2**). Push the new loop of Bs to the left so it rests on top of the previous loop.

3 Repeat step 2 to reach the desired rope length.

FIGURE 1　　　FIGURE 2

Varying the spiral rope

· Make loops with an 11º, a 4 mm pearl or crystal, and an 11º.

· Make loops with an 11º, a 6 mm offset-hole lentil bead, and an 11º.

· Make a double spiral in which a second set of loops is added in the groove created by the first set of loops.

RUSSIAN SPIRAL

Russian spiral is a variant of tubular netting. It is usually stitched with beads in two sizes — often two sizes of seed beads, or seed beads and either bugle beads or crystals — resulting in alternating stripes circling the tube.

1 On a comfortable length of thread, pick up a repeating pattern of two 11° seed beads and an 8° seed bead three times, and tie the beads into a ring with a square knot, leaving a 6-in. (15 cm) tail. Sew through the first 11° again **(figure 3)**.

2 Pick up an 8° and two 11°s, and sew through the 11° right after the next 8° **(figure 4, a–b)**. Repeat **(b–c)**. Repeat again, and step up through the first two beads added in this round **(c–d)**.

3 Repeat step 2 **(figure 5)** for the desired rope length.

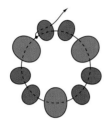

FIGURE 3

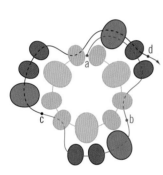

FIGURE 4

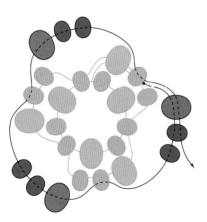

FIGURE 5

Using different combinations of beads

Make a variation with two 15°s substituted for the 11°s and a 3 mm bugle for the 8°.

Make a pearl variation with three 11°s instead of two and a 4 mm pearl instead of the 8°.

Make a multicolor variation with three 11°s instead of two, and a rotating pattern of a 4 mm crystal, a 4 mm glass bead, or a 4 mm pearl instead of the 8°s.

AFRICAN HELIX

African helix is also a variant of netting, but instead of adding stitches by sewing through existing beads, the working thread is looped around the thread in the previous round. This results in "spine" beads that pop out from the "background" beads.

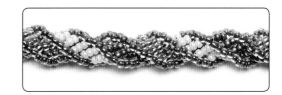

1 On a comfortable length of thread, pick up three color A 11º seed beads, one color D 11º seed bead, three color B 11º seed beads, one D, three color C 11º seed beads, and one D, leaving a 6-in. (15 cm) tail. Tie the beads into a ring with a square knot (**photo a**). Slide the ring over a cylindrical support form, like a knitting needle, with the As to the right of the knot, and tape the tail to the form above the ring.

2 Work the next stitch vertically, from top to bottom: Pick up three As and two Ds, and pass the needle down through the ring between the beads and the form (**photo b**). Guide the thread between the third A and the first D, grasp both the loop thread and the tail, and tug gently until it snaps into place between the A and D and a small loop has formed below the ring. Pull the beads snug (**photo c**).

3 Repeat step 2 using Bs instead of As and guiding the thread between the set of three Bs and the following D (**photo d**). Repeat again using Cs instead of As.

4 Continue as in steps 2 and 3, dropping the needle between the third background bead and the first spine bead in the next loop until the rope is the desired length. After you have an inch or so of beadwork, you can remove it from the support if desired.

Try your hand at these variations

· Use a single color for the background and a different single color for the spines.

· Use a single color for the background and alternating spine colors to make dots.

· Use a single color for the background and multiple spine colors.

· Substitute a 4 mm bead for each set of background beads to create a look similar to Russian spiral.

CHENILLE STITCH

You'll love the beautiful results you get from this fast and easy stitch. Chenille stitch (meaning "caterpillar" in French) is essentially a combination of netting and herringbone stitches. When completed, it has the same basic look as netting but because of the thread path used to create it, it is sturdier and tighter. It is a fun and easy stitch to learn, and you can create lots of varied looks simply by using different beads. Chenille stitch is usually seen in its tubular form, but flat designs are also possible — we'll show you both.

MATERIALS

samples
- assorted seed beads and accent beads
- Fireline, 6 lb. test
- beading needles, #11

TECHNIQUES
- beading fundamentals: attaching a stop bead, ending and adding thread (p. 20)

Color A: 2 mm fire-polished beads; Color B: 11º seed beads

Color A: 3 x 4 mm rondelles; Color B: 11º seed beads

Color A: 3 mm melon beads; Color B: 11º seed beads

Color A: 4 mm round crystals; Color B: 11º seed beads

Color A: 4 mm pinch beads; Color B: 11º seed beads

Color A: 4 mm round beads; Color B: 11º seed beads

8º s in two colors

Color A: 8º seed beads; Color B: 3 mm melon beads

Color A: 4 mm bicone crystals; Color B: 11º seed beads

Color A: 4 mm fire-polished beads; Color B: 11º seed beads

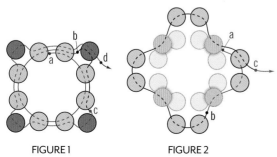

FIGURE 1   FIGURE 2

TUBULAR CHENILLE STITCH

To learn this stitch, use two colors of 8º seed beads (colors A and B).

1 On a comfortable length of thread, pick up eight color A 8º seed beads (any even number will work, but eight is good for learning). Leaving a 6-in. (15 cm) tail, tie the beads into a ring with a square knot, and sew through the first A (**figure 1, a–b**). This is round 1.

2 Work in rounds as follows:

Round 2: Pick up one color B 8º seed bead, and sew through the next two As in the ring (**b–c**). Repeat this stitch three times, and step up through the first B added in this round (**c–d**).

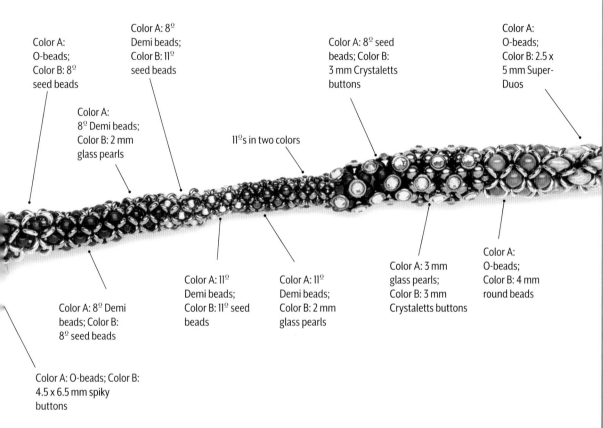

Color A: O-beads; Color B: 8º seed beads

Color A: 8º Demi beads; Color B: 11º seed beads

Color A: 8º Demi beads; Color B: 2 mm glass pearls

11ºs in two colors

Color A: 8º seed beads; Color B: 3 mm Crystaletts buttons

Color A: O-beads; Color B: 2.5 x 5 mm Super-Duos

Color A: 11º Demi beads; Color B: 11º seed beads

Color A: 11º Demi beads; Color B: 2 mm glass pearls

Color A: 3 mm glass pearls; Color B: 3 mm Crystaletts buttons

Color A: O-beads; Color B: 4 mm round beads

Color A: 8º Demi beads; Color B: 8º seed beads

Color A: O-beads; Color B: 4.5 x 6.5 mm spiky buttons

Round 3: Pick up two As, and sew through the next B **(figure 2, a–b)**. Repeat this stitch three times, and step up through the first A added in this round **(b–c)**.
Round 4: Pick up a B, and sew through the next two As **(figure 3, a–b)**. With this stitch, you are inserting a B between the pair of As in the stitch below. Repeat this stitch three times to complete the round, and step up through the first B added in this round **(b–c)**.
3 Repeat rounds 3 and 4 for the desired length, ending with round 3 (all As).
4 To close the end of the tube, sew through the final round of As **(figure 4)**. End the thread.

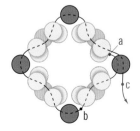

FIGURE 3

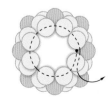

FIGURE 4

FIGURE 5

FIGURE 6

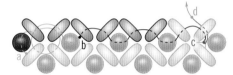

FIGURE 7

FIGURE 8

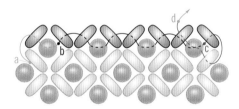

FIGURE 9

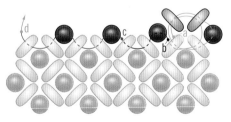

FIGURE 10

FLAT CHENILLE STITCH

Flat chenille stitch is a bit trickier than the tubular form because you have to keep switching direction, rather than simply spiraling around. For this version, we used 8° Demi beads as the As and 2 mm glass pearls as the Bs.

1 On a comfortable length of thread, attach a stop bead, leaving a 6-in. (15 cm) tail.
2 Work in rows as follows:
Row 1: Pick up an A and a B, then a repeating pattern of two As and a B three times, and then an A, a B, and two As. Sew through the last four As again, skipping the Bs (**figure 5**).
Row 2: Pick up a B, and sew back through the next two As in the previous row (**figure 6, a–b**). Repeat twice (**b–c**).
Row 3: Pick up a B and two As, sew back through the next two As in row 1, and sew through the two new As again and the following B in row 2 (**figure 7, a–b**). Pick up two As, and sew through the next B. Repeat this stitch once, and sew through the two As that were added to the end of row 1 (**b–c**). Sew under the thread bridge between the two adjacent rows of As, and sew back through the last A your thread exited (**c–d**).
Row 4: Pick up a B, and sew through the next two As in the previous row. Repeat this stitch three times, noting that you'll sew through only one A in the last stitch of the row (**figure 8**).
Row 5: Pick up an A, and sew through the next B (**figure 9, a–b**). Pick up two As, and sew through the next B. Repeat this stitch twice (**b–c**). Pick up an A, and sew back through the A below, the adjacent B in row 4, and the second-to-last A added in this row (**c–d**).
Row 6: Pick up two As and a B, and sew through the two adjacent As in the previous row. Continue through the two new As, skip the new B, and sew through the two As in the previous row again (**figure 10, a–b**). Pick up a B, and sew through the next two As (**b–c**). Repeat this stitch twice (**c–d**).
3 Repeat rows 3–6 for the desired length, ending with row 4, and end the thread.

Origins

To the best of our knowledge, chenille stitch was created in the mid-2000s by Geneviève Liebaert, known on her blog at the time as Sereine. Not long after posting her chenille stitch tutorial, Sereine stopped beading, though some of her work still exists on a French beading forum. Some time later, another beader, Sara Spoltore, not being familiar with Sereine's tutorial, also "invented" the technique and made a YouTube video showing how to do it, which has become very popular. In later correspondence, Sara informed us that though she came up with the stitch independently, she was unwilling to claim the technique as her own because Sereine had already invented it. Thanks to both these talented beaders for sharing this technique with the beading world!

CHEVRON CHAIN

Take a cue from netting to create an elegant stitch. Chevron chain takes its name from the alternating Vs and inverted Vs that make up the center strip. Sometimes referred to as zigzag stitch, it is a variation of netting.

Historically, netting variations can be found in most cultures around the world from Africa to Asia and the Americas. Cultures that worked with seed beads developed their own bead-netting and bead-weaving techniques, and there is some resemblance between stitches. For example, chevron chain looks similar to triangle weave, which is related to right-angle weave.

The stitches differ in the arrangement of their shared beads and the direction of the thread path. As a relative of netting, chevron chain can be thought of as a series of linked turns.

MATERIALS
samples
- **1–2 g** 11º seed beads in each of 3 colors: A, B, C
- assorted beads, such as: 12 mm bugles, 6 mm bicone crystals, 6 mm vintage glass beads, 6 mm glass pearls, 6 mm jade beads, 4–5 mm bicone crystals, 4 mm glass pearls, 4 mm round crystals, 3 mm crystal rondelles, 8º seed beads, and 11º hex-cut seed beads
- Fireline, 6 lb. test, or nylon beading thread, size D
- beading needles, #10 or #12

TECHNIQUES
- beading fundamentals: attaching a stop bead (p. 20)

You can change the look of chevron chain by changing bead sizes and bead counts to create a tightly woven piece or a loose, open look. It helps to think of a chevron chain stitch as having three basic elements: a pair of diagonal strips (the green beads in **figures 1–3**), a connector at the point of the strips' intersection (the gray beads), and a bridge joining the outer edges of the strips (the yellow-orange beads).

To change the width of a stitch, increase or decrease the size or number of beads in the bridge. You can change the height of the row by increasing or decreasing the size or number of beads in the connector or diagonal strips. Vary chevron chain by changing colors and experimenting with their arrangement. Try using different beads or bead counts on the top and bottom bridges.

While chevron chain is normally worked as a single chain, you can add rows to create a panel. You can work tubular chevron chain by connecting the ends. Once you are familiar with the stitch, you can add embellishments and create your own variations.

SINGLE CHEVRON CHAIN
1 Attach a stop bead to a comfortable length of thread, leaving a 6-in. (15 cm) tail.
2 Pick up three color A seed beads, three color B seed beads, three As, three color C seed beads, three As, and three Bs (**figure 1, a–b**). Sew back through the first three As (**b–c**).
3 Pick up three Cs, three As, and three Bs, and sew back through the last three As added in the previous stitch (**figure 2**).
4 Repeat step 3 to the desired length (**figure 3**). The direction of the Vs will alternate with each stitch.

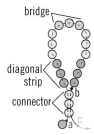
FIGURE 1

FIGURE 2

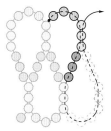
FIGURE 3

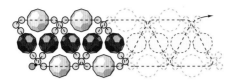

FIGURE 4

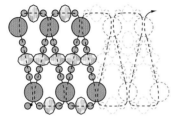

FIGURE 5

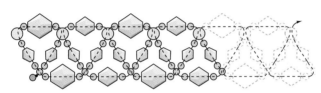

FIGURE 6

SINGLE VARIATIONS

Figures 4, 5, and 6 show just a few of the possible variations of single chevron chain, all of which follow the basic principle of using a connector, a pair of diagonal strips, and a bridge. In "Single chevron chain," the group of three As represents a connector, the Bs represent the diagonal strips, and the Cs represent a bridge.

To work the first stitch, pick up a connector, a diagonal strip, a connector, a bridge, a connector, and a diagonal strip, and sew through the first connector. In each subsequent stitch, pick up a bridge, a connector, and a diagonal strip, and sew through the previous connector. Once you have the basic pattern, you can create variations.

In **figure 4**, large beads create a dense stitch. A seed bead is used as the connector; a seed bead, 4 mm round crystal, and seed bead are used for each diagonal strip; and a seed bead, a 6 mm glass bead, and a seed bead are used as the bridge.

In **figure 5**, more beads in the diagonal strip add height. A 6 mm pearl is used as the connector; two seed beads, a 3 mm rondelle, and two seed beads are used for each diagonal strip; and a seed bead, a 3 mm rondelle, and a seed bead are used as the bridge.

In **figure 6**, larger beads in the bridge add width.

The connector alternates between a seed bead at the bottom and a 4 mm pearl at the top; each diagonal strip is made of a seed bead, a 4 mm bicone crystal, and a seed bead; and the bridges alternate between a 5 mm and a 6 mm bicone crystal with a seed bead on both sides of each crystal.

ADDING ROWS

1 Follow steps 1–4 of "Single chevron chain."

2 With your thread exiting a bottom A, sew through the following three Cs, three As, three Bs, three As, and three Cs at the top (**figure 7, a–b**).

3 Pick up three As, three Bs, three As, three Cs, three As, and three Bs. Sew back through the first three As added and the three Cs in the previous row your thread exited at the start of this step (**b–c**).

4 Pick up three As and three Bs, and sew through the adjacent three As added in the previous step (**c–d**).

5 Pick up three Cs, three As, and three Bs, and sew through the three As added in the previous step and the next three Cs in the previous row (**d–e**).

6 Repeat steps 4 and 5 to the desired length.

CONNECTING THE ENDS INTO A RING

1 Follow steps 1–4 of "Single chevron chain," ending with an even number of stitches and the same number of bridges along the top and bottom edges.

2 Pick up three Cs, and sew through the corresponding three As in the first stitch (**figure 8, a–b**).

3 Pick up three Bs, and sew through the corresponding three As in the previous stitch (**b–c**).

4 Pick up three Cs, and sew through the corresponding three As in the first stitch (**c–d**).

TUBULAR CHEVRON CHAIN

You can create tubular chevron chain two ways:

· Follow the steps in "Single chevron chain" to the desired length, "Adding rows" to the desired height, and "Connecting the ends" to create the tube.

· Follow the steps in "Single chevron chain" to the desired length, "Connecting the ends" to create the tube, and "Adding rows" to the desired length of the tube.

FIGURE 7

FIGURE 8

Try different bead arrangements

· Use the same beads, but alternate their placement for two very different looks.

· Alternate bead sizes for the top and bottom bridges to form a curve.

ST. PETERSBURG CHAIN

Worked as a single or doubled chain, St. Petersburg chain has gained popularity around the world. Originally from Russia, St. Petersburg chain has become more and more fashionable with beaders around the globe. Its unusual, asymmetrical technique and stepped chain form has made it a favorite among experienced beaders for decades, and more exciting design possibilities are being explored as beaders discover the stitch.

St. Petersburg chain has been in the background of the beading scene for awhile, first appearing in the wider world in the form of leaves and ornaments, and more recently becoming popular for chains and bezels. Many dedicated beaders in the Western world taught themselves the stitch by studying the illustrations in Russian-language beading books, such as *The Art of Beading* by Maya Anufrieva. Eastern European and Asian beaders have been exploring the possibilities of this stitch for a bit longer.

The stitch can be worked with just about any type of bead, but when learning, it's easiest to start with two types or two colors of seed beads.

MATERIALS

samples
- **1–2 g** 11º seed beads, in 2 colors: A, B
- Fireline, 6 lb. test, or nylon beading thread, size D
- beading needles, #11

TECHNIQUES
- beading fundamentals: attaching a stop bead, conditioning thread, ending and adding thread (p. 20)

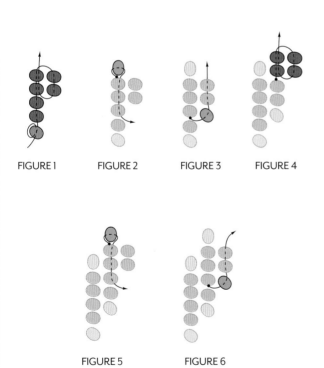

FIGURE 1   FIGURE 2   FIGURE 3   FIGURE 4

FIGURE 5   FIGURE 6

SINGLE ST. PETERSBURG CHAIN

1 Attach a stop bead to a comfortable length of thread.

2 Pick up six A seed beads. Sew through the third and fourth As again, so the fifth and sixth beads form an adjacent column (**figure 1**).

3 Pick up a B seed bead, and sew back through the next three As in the column (**figure 2**).

4 Pick up a B, and sew through the two As in the newest column (**figure 3**).

5 Pick up four As, and sew through the first two As just picked up, sliding the four beads tight to the existing chain (**figure 4**).

6 Pick up a B, and sew back through the next three As in the column (**figure 5**).

7 Pick up a B, and sew through the two As in the new column (**figure 6**).

8 Repeat steps 5–7 to the desired length.

FIGURE 7

FIGURE 8

FIGURE 9

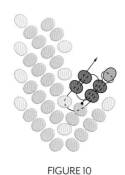

FIGURE 10

DOUBLE ST. PETERSBURG CHAIN

For double St. Petersburg chain, work one side of the chain as in single St. Petersburg chain, then work the second side using the tail, or a second length of thread.

1 Attach a stop bead in the center of the thread. Wind up the long tail on a card or bobbin, so it stays out of the way as you work the first half of the chain.

2 Work in St. Petersburg chain as in steps 2–8 of "Single St. Petersburg chain." Attach a stop bead to temporarily secure the thread.

3 Remove the stop bead from the starting end of the chain. Pick up six As, and sew through the third and fourth As again, as in step 2 **(figure 7)**.

4 Pick up a B, and sew back through the next three As in the column **(figure 8)**.

5 Sew through the adjacent B from the first side of the chain and the two As in the newest column of the second side **(figure 9)**. Pull tight.

6 Pick up four As, and sew through the first two As again. Pick up a B, and sew back through the next three As in the column. Sew through the next B in the first chain, and through the two As in the newest column **(figure 10)**. Repeat this step to the end of the chain.

LOOMWORK

The process of weaving beads into the warp and weft on fiber looms predates written history. In North America, native peoples were weaving bands of beads before European settlers arrived. They first used beads made from shell, clay, bone, wood, and other natural materials. Their looms were also made of natural materials — small tree boughs, cured animal hides and sinews, and plant fibers. Needles were made from bone. These lightweight looms were easy to hold in one's lap.

The European introduction of metal tools and iron needles contributed to changes in bead looms. When European traders introduced glass seed beads in the 17th century, Native American bead artists incorporated this new material into their designs. Brightly colored native beadwork decorated

ceremonial vessels, wampum belts, clothing, footwear, tools, and weapons.

It was also worn as jewelry and hair ties. Native weavers developed a number of loomwork techniques, many of which were based on basket-weaving, braiding, and handheld finger-weaving methods. They perfected the single- and double-strand square weave and variations of these methods. The

single-strand square weave is similar to today's loomwork technique in which a single weft passes through the same row of beads twice.

Today, the bead loom has many variations in size, framework construction, and materials. The basics of beadweaving on a loom, however, remain the same.

MATERIALS
- 1–2 g 11° seed beads, in multiple colors
- Fireline, 6 lb. test, or nylon beading thread, size D
- needles, #10 or #12
- loom

TECHNIQUES
- beading fundamentals: attaching a stop bead, conditioning thread, ending and adding thread (p. 20)

WARPING A TRADITIONAL LOOM

1 Tie the end of a spool of thread to a screw or a hook at one end of the loom.

2 Guide the thread between two coils of the spring and across to the other end of the loom. Guide the thread between the corresponding coils of the opposite spring, and wrap it around the screw or hook at this end. Go back over the spring, placing the thread in the next coil. Cross over to the first end of the loom, placing the thread in the corresponding coil, and wrap it around the screw or hook.

note If you are using beads that are larger than 11° seed beads, you may want to skip one or more coils between warp threads.

FIGURE 1

3 Continue wrapping the thread between coils, keeping the thread a bead's width apart (**figure 1**), until you have one more warp thread than the number of beads in the width of the pattern. Keep the tension even, but not too tight. Tie the last warp thread to a hook or screw on the loom, then cut the thread from the spool.

LOOMWORK

WEAVING THE PATTERN

1 Tie the end of a 1-yd. (.9 m) length of thread to the first warp near the top or bottom of the loom.

2 Bring the thread behind the warp threads. String the first row of beads, from left to right **(figure 2)**, and slide them to the knot.

3 Push the beads up between the warp threads with your finger **(figure 3)**.

4 Sew back through the beads, keeping the needle on top of the warp threads **(figure 4)**.

5 Repeat steps 2–4 to complete the pattern, ending and adding thread as needed.

6 Once you complete the last row, secure the working weft thread by weaving it into the beadwork.

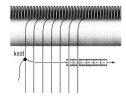

FIGURE 2   FIGURE 3

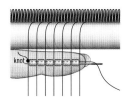

FIGURE 4

DECREASING

To decrease, sew under the end warp thread of the row you just completed, and sew back through the beads you'll omit in the decrease row. Wrap the working thread around the warp thread that will be the left edge of the decrease row. Pick up the beads needed for the decrease row, and position them. At the other end, skip the warps to the right of the beads that will be omitted, and sew back through the newly added beads **(figure 5)**.

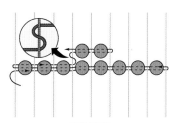

FIGURE 5

FINISHING THE LOOMWORK

1 To remove the beadwork from the loom, carefully cut the warp threads as close to the screw or hook as possible.

2 Starting with the end warp on one side, thread a needle, and sew through the first bead in the end row. Sew through the corresponding bead in the adjacent row, the first bead again, and the next bead or two in the row. Repeat, moving down the end row. At the end of the row, sew into the bead-work, and end the thread **(figure 6)**.

3 Repeat with the remaining warp threads, moving away from the end row as you end each thread.

4 Repeat on the other end with the remaining warp threads, making sure to maintain even tension throughout the strip of loomwork. If you pull too hard, the beads will bunch up.

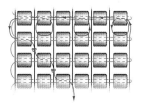

FIGURE 6

BEAD CROCHET

The slip stitch method of tubular bead crochet is a popular technique often used for making beautiful beaded ropes. Learn how you can make a slip stitch rope and how to join the ends invisibly.

MATERIALS

sample
- **1–2 g** 11º or 8º seed beads, in multiple colors
- yarn or other fiber
- big-eye needle
- steel crochet hook

TECHNIQUES
- beading fundamentals: attaching a stop bead, conditioning thread, ending and adding thread (p. 20)

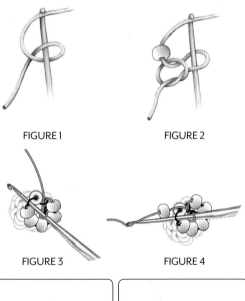

FIGURE 1

FIGURE 2

FIGURE 3

FIGURE 4

a

b

c

d

BEAD-CROCHET ROPES

A multitude of fibers can be used in bead crochet, which is worked with a steel crochet hook. You'll need to experiment to find your preferences. While learning bead crochet, you may find it helpful to work in a repeating pattern so you can easily see what stitch your hook should be going into. In the instructions below, we show a five-around rope using a different bead color for each stitch in the round.

1 String the beads for your project onto the cord, keeping in mind that the first beads strung will be the last beads worked. For learning purposes, string 3–4 ft. (.9–1.2 m) of beads in a repeating pattern of five colors. Do not cut the cord from the spool — wind the strung beads around the spool, and unwind them as you work.

2 Begin with a slip knot: Leaving a 10-in. (25 cm) tail, make a loop in the cord, crossing the spool end over the tail. Insert the hook in the loop, yarn over (**figure 1**), and pull the cord through the loop.

3 Work a bead chain stitch: Slide a bead down to the hook, yarn over the hook (**figure 2**), and pull the cord through the loop. Repeat to make a total of five bead chain stitches. The bead chain should curl into the shape of a comma (**photo a**).

4 Use a bead slip stitch to join the chain into a ring: Insert the hook to the left of the first bead in the chain, flipping the bead to the right of the hook (**photo b**). Slide the next bead down to the hook, and yarn over (**photo c**). Pull the cord through both the stitch in the previous round and the loop on the hook (**photo d**). This is the first stitch of the next round.

5 Continue working in bead slip stitch: Insert the hook to the left of the next bead in the previous round, and flip that bead to the right **(figure 3)**. Slide a bead down to the hook, yarn over **(figure 4)**, and pull the cord through both the stitch in the previous round and the loop on the hook. Repeat around the ring, working each stitch into the loop that attaches the next bead in the previous round.

If you used a different color for each bead in the round, each stitch will be worked in a stitch with the same color bead. As you work, notice that the beads in the working round sit perpendicular to the beads in the previous rounds. They will be flipped into place when you work the next round. Work to the desired length. Cut the cord, leaving a 6-in. (15 cm) tail, and pull the cord through the last stitch.

note If you have trouble obtaining the correct tension, try the following: If the tension is too tight, use a hook one size larger. If you are crocheting too loosely, use a hook one size smaller.

INVISIBLE JOIN

Beaders have found a number of ways to join the ends of a crochet rope. The following method can be used with a slip stitch bead-crochet rope of any bead count diameter. The instructions below refer to a five-around rope, but if you make a six-around rope, for example, adjust the counts in the instructions accordingly.

1 To bury the ending tail, thread a tapestry needle, and carefully sew into the middle of the rope, exiting between two beads several rounds into the work. Sew in and out of the rope several times, crossing over the cord within the rope without sewing through any beads, and trim the cord as close to the beadwork as possible.

2 Thread a tapestry needle on the beginning tail, which is exiting the first stitch in the first round. Identify the five beads added in the final round and the five beads in the first round. The beads in the final round lie sideways because they haven't yet been locked in place.

3 Line up the ends of the rope, aligning the pattern. On the tail end of the rope, sew under the loop of the fifth bead from the end. Flip the bead to the right as you would while crocheting **(photo e)**. Notice that this bead is the same color as the one your cord just came from at the other end of the rope.

4 At the beginning of the rope, sew under the loop of the second bead in the first round **(photo f)**, sewing toward the third bead.

5 Cross over to the tail end again, and sew under the fourth bead from the end of the round **(photo g)**.

6 Continue working back and forth between the ends, flipping the beads in the final round and matching up the pattern. Snug up the ends as you work. After you've flipped the last bead on the tail end, sew under the first bead at the beginning end again. End the tail as in step 1.

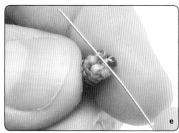

 TIP Size 20 crochet cotton creates the tight drape that's perfect for a bangle.

COMBINING STITCHES

Certain basic stitches use combinations as part of their construction. For example, ladder stitch is often used as a base row or round for brick stitch and herringbone stitch. This type of combination is called a "functional combination" because it occurs out of necessity instead of as a design element.

Sometimes within a design, stitches are combined when separate components worked in different stitches are joined to create a larger piece. Component combinations are a good place to start when you want to begin designing using multiple stitches. Once you are comfortable with all the basic stitches, you may find it easier to combine or switch between stitches within a single design.

MATERIALS
- **1–2 g** 11º seed beads
- Fireline, 6 lb. test, or nylon beading thread, size D
- beading needles, #11

TECHNIQUES
- beading fundamentals: attaching a stop bead, conditioning thread, ending and adding thread (p. 20)
- peyote stitch (p. 24)
- ladder stitch (p. 36)
- herringbone stitch (p. 42)
- right-angle weave (p. 46)

1 PEYOTE STITCH/ HERRINGBONE STITCH

1 Pick up 11 As. Work a total of six rows of odd-count peyote stitch using As **(figure 1, a–b)**.
2 Switch from peyote to herringbone: Work a row of peyote stitch, picking up two Cs per stitch. When making the odd-count turn at the end of the row, sew back through only the last C picked up in the end stitch **(b–c)**. Work a row of herringbone stitch off the previous row using Cs **(c–d)**. Work three more rows of herringbone stitch using Cs **(d–e)**.
3 Switch from herringbone to peyote: Work a row of herringbone stitch, picking up only one A per stitch. When you reach the end of the row, sew back through the last A added **(e–f)**. Pick up an A, and sew through the next A in the previous row. Continue in peyote stitch to complete the row **(f–g)**. Work four more rows of peyote stitch using As **(g–h)**.

2 RIGHT-ANGLE WEAVE/ PEYOTE STITCH

1 Work a row of five right-angle weave stitches using Bs **(figure 2, a–b)**. Add two more rows using Bs. Sew through the last stitch to exit an end B **(b–c)**.
2 Switch from right-angle weave to peyote stitch: Work a row of odd-count peyote stitch using As **(c–d)**. Work a row of odd-count peyote stitch off the previous row using As. Work three more rows of odd-count peyote stitch using As **(d–e)**.
3 Switch from peyote stitch to right-angle weave: Work a row of odd-count peyote stitch using Bs, and exit the last B added **(e–f)**. Pick up three Bs, and sew through the B your thread exited at the start of this stitch **(f–g)**. Continue in right-angle weave to complete the row, picking up two Bs per stitch **(g–h)**. Work two more rows of right-angle weave using Bs **(h–i)**.

3 HERRINGBONE STITCH/ RIGHT-ANGLE WEAVE

1 Make a ladder stitch base 10 Cs long **(figure 3, a–b)**. Work four rows of herringbone stitch using Cs **(b–c)**.
2 Switch from herringbone to right-angle weave: Work a row of herringbone stitch, picking up only one A per stitch. When you reach the end of the row, sew back through the last A added **(c–d)**. Pick up three As, and sew through the A your thread exited at the start of this stitch. Continue working across the row in right-angle weave **(d–e)**. Work two more rows using As, and exit the end A in the last stitch of the row **(e–f)**.
3 Switch from right-angle weave to herringbone: Pick up two Cs, and sew through the A your thread exited at the start of this stitch **(f–g)**. Exit the end A in the next stitch of the previous row **(g–h)**. Repeat **(h–i)** to complete the row. Step up through the end C **(i–j)**. Work a row of herringbone off the As in the previous row **(j–k)**. Continue **(k–l)**.

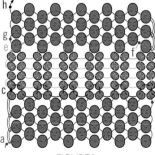

FIGURE 1

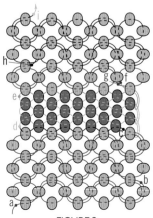

FIGURE 2

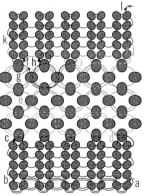

FIGURE 3

projects

Paved in goldstone bracelet

Embellish a peyote band of expertly blended colors with gemstone chips and crystal fringe.

designed by Ryan Messinger

MATERIALS

bracelet 7½ in. (19.1cm)

- **1** 18 mm (large) Bali shank button (TierraCast, antique copper-plated)
- **40** 4–10 mm gemstone chips (goldstone)
- **56** 3 mm bicone crystals (Swarovski, "Southwest flair" designer blend)
- **18 g** 8° seed beads (Toho, "Southwest sunset" designer blend)
- **1 g** 15° seed beads (Toho 421, gold-lustered transparent pink)
- Fireline, 4 lb. test
- beading needles, #11

TECHNIQUES

- beading fundamentals: ending and adding thread, attaching a stop bead (p. 20)
- peyote stitch: flat even-count (p. 24)

1 Separate out the purple beads from your 8° seed bead blend. Keep the remaining colors mixed.

2 On a comfortable length of thread, attach a stop bead, leaving a 10-in. (25 cm) tail. Pick up 12 purple 8°s **(figure 1, a–b)**.

3 Work a row of flat even-count peyote stitch, using a purple 8° for the first stitch and any other 8°s from the blend for the next five stitches **(b–c)**. Repeat for a total of 112 rows or to the desired length, ending and adding thread as needed.

note Remember to start each row with a purple 8°, and aim for a random mix of colors for the remainder of the row.

End by working two more rows with purple 8°s **(d–e)**.

4 To make the button clasp: Sew through the beadwork to the sixth row from the end, and exit the third 8° in the row. Pick up an 18 mm shank button, and sew through the fourth 8° in the row.

note In figure 1, the third and fourth 8°s in the sixth row from the end are each outlined in red.

Retrace the thread path of the button connection at least twice, and end the working thread.

5 To make the clasp loop: Remove the stop bead from the tail, and sew through the beadwork to exit the third 8° in row 1. Pick up 26 purple 8°s, or enough to fit around your button. Sew back through the first 8° added in this step, and continue through the fourth 8° in the row **(figure 2, a–b)**. Retrace

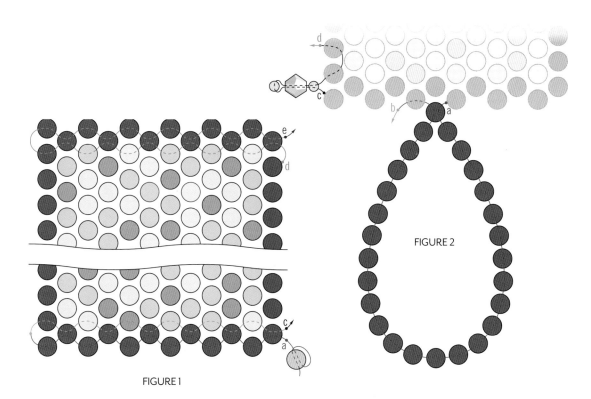

FIGURE 1

FIGURE 2

the thread path of the loop at least twice, and end the tail.

6 Add a comfortable length of thread to the beadwork, and exit the first purple 8º along one edge. Pick up a 15º seed bead, a 3 mm bicone crystal, and a 15º, and sew back through the crystal and first 15º added. Continue through the next 8º along the edge and the following 8º **(c–d)**. Repeat this stitch for the length of the band, aiming for a random mix of crystal colors. Sew through the beadwork to exit the first purple 8º along the other edge, and work the same stitch along this edge. End and add thread as needed.

7 Sew through the beadwork to the center of the band, exiting an 8º approximately 2 mm from the button or the loop, depending on which end you're working on. Pick up a gemstone chip and a 15º, sew back through the chip, and continue through the same 8º in the band.

8 Sew through the beadwork to another 8º just to the right of the center of the band, exiting 3–5 mm from the previous chip. Pick up a chip and a 15º, sew back through the chip, and

continue through the same 8º in the band. Repeat to add a second chip to the left of the center of the band. Continue adding pairs of chips down the center of the band, selecting chips of differing shapes and sizes for interest. End with a single chip approximately 2 mm from the button or the loop, as in step 7. End the thread.

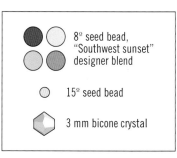

		8º seed bead, "Southwest sunset" designer blend
	○	15º seed bead
	◇	3 mm bicone crystal

TIP Use this same technique to stitch an ultra-wide cuff with a double button-and-loop closure.

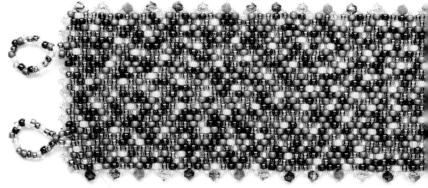

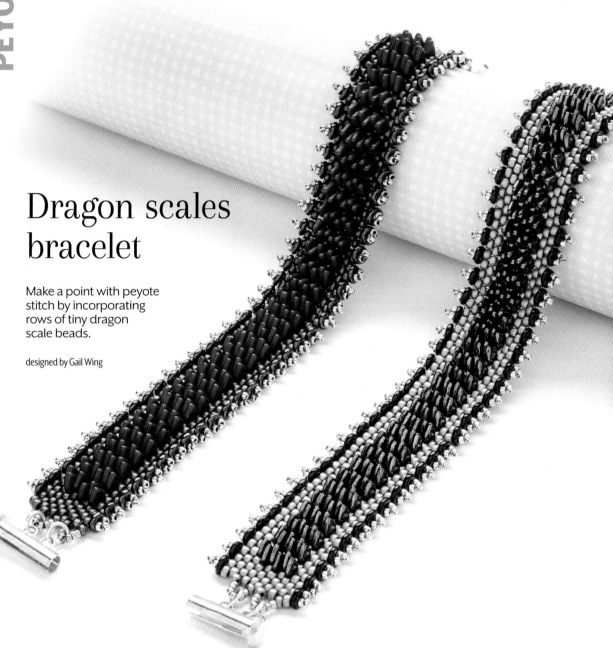

Dragon scales bracelet

Make a point with peyote stitch by incorporating rows of tiny dragon scale beads.

designed by Gail Wing

BAND

1 On a comfortable length of thread, attach a stop bead, leaving a 12-in. (30 cm) tail. Pick up 10 11º seed beads.
2 Using 11ºs, work in flat even-count peyote stitch until you have a total of six rows.

3 For the next row, work as follows: One stitch with an 11º, three stitches with a dragon scale bead for each stitch, and one stitch with an 11º (**figure 1, a–b**). Work a second row **in** the same manner (**b–c**).

<u>note</u> **As you add the scale beads in the second row, you will be sewing through the scale beads added in the previous row.**

4 Work a row with 11ºs. Again, you will be sewing through the scale beads added in the previous row, which may be difficult to visually differentiate from

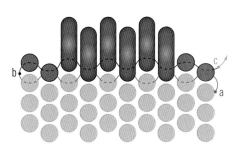

FIGURE 1

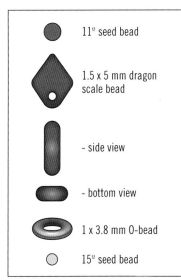

11º seed bead

1.5 x 5 mm dragon scale bead

- side view

- bottom view

1 x 3.8 mm O-bead

15º seed bead

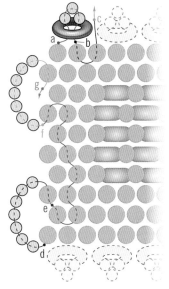

FIGURE 2

MATERIALS

red bracelet 7 in. (18 cm)
- **198** 1.5 x 5 mm dragon scale beads (lava red)
- **72** 1 x 3.8 mm O-beads (jet lila Vega luster)
- **5 g** 11º seed beads (Toho 46F, frosted oxblood)
- **1 g** 15º seed beads (Miyuki 190, nickel plated)
- **1** 2-hole slide clasp (silver)
- **4** 6 mm jump rings (silver)
- Fireline, 6 lb. test
- beading needles, #11
- **2** pairs of chainnose, flatnose, and/or bentnose pliers

gray bracelet colors
- 1.5 x 5 mm dragon scale beads (hematite)
- 1 x 3.8 mm O-beads (jet)
- 11º seed beads (Toho 566, matte pewter)
- 15º seed beads (Miyuki 190, nickel-plated)

Techniques Used
- beading fundamentals: attaching a stop bead, ending and adding thread, opening and closing jump rings (p. 20)
- peyote stitch: flat even-count (p. 24)

the first row of scale beads at this point. Flip your work to the back to help you see where you are stitching, and remember to always skip a scale bead before sewing through the next one.

5 Work another row with 11ºs, this time sewing through the 11ºs in the previous row.

6 Repeat steps 3–5 for the desired length, ending and adding thread as needed. For a 7-in. (18 cm) finished bracelet, work until you have a total of 33 scale-bead ridges.

7 Work four more rows with 11ºs for a total of six rows on this end of the band. End the working thread but not the tail.

EDGING

1 Add a comfortable length of thread to the band, and exit the first 11º along one edge. Rotate your work so this edge is at the top.

2 Pick up an O-bead and three 15º seed beads, and sew back through the O-bead to form a picot (**figure 2, a–b**). Sew down through the next 11º along the edge and up through the following 11º (**b–c**).

3 Repeat step 2 along this edge of the band. Sew through the beadwork to exit the first 11º along the other edge, and repeat step 2 along this edge.

CLASP

1 Sew through the band on the end opposite the tail to exit the end up-bead along one edge, making sure your needle is pointing away from the band (**figure 2, point d**). Pick up seven 15ºs, and sew through the next up-bead as shown to form a loop (**d–e**). Sew through the beadwork to exit the second up-bead from the loop (**e–f**), and form another loop (**f–g**). Retrace the thread path through the loops, and end the working thread.

2 Remove the stop bead from the tail, and work as in step 1 on the other end of the band.

3 Open two jump rings, and attach half of the clasp to the loops at one end of the band. Repeat on the other end of the band.

Heart of stone necklace

Combine gemstones, copper components, pearls, and leather for an earthy look.

designed by Marla Salezze

MATERIALS
adjustable necklace 27 in. (69 cm)
- gemstone beads (bronzite; dakotastones.com)
  - **1** 15 x 30 mm rectangle
  - **1** 15 mm square
- **2** 6 mm crystal pearls (Swarovski, gold)
- 11º cylinder beads (Miyuki)
  - **1 g** color A (DB0108, cinnamon gold luster)
  - **1 g** color B (DB1051, matte brown)
- Nunn Design components (antique copper; nunndesign.com)
  - **1** 44.6 x 25.6 mm oval double-loop grande connector
  - **1** 15.3 x 12.8 mm rustic heart charm
  - **1** 13 x 11.1 mm medium channel bead
  - **1** 6.1 x 11.1 mm small channel bead
  - **3** 11.3 mm large rope jump rings
  - **3** 9 mm textured circle jump rings
  - **1** 2-in. (5 cm) head pin
  - **1** 2-in. (5 cm) eye pin
- 30 in. (76 cm) 5 mm deerskin lace
- Fireline, 6 lb. test
- beading needles, #10
- **2** pairs of chainnose, flatnose, and/or bentnose pliers
- roundnose pliers
- wire cutters

TECHNIQUES
- beading fundamentals: attaching a stop bead, ending thread, wrapped loop, opening and closing jump rings, overhand knot (p. 20)
- peyote stitch: flat even-count, zipping up (p. 24)

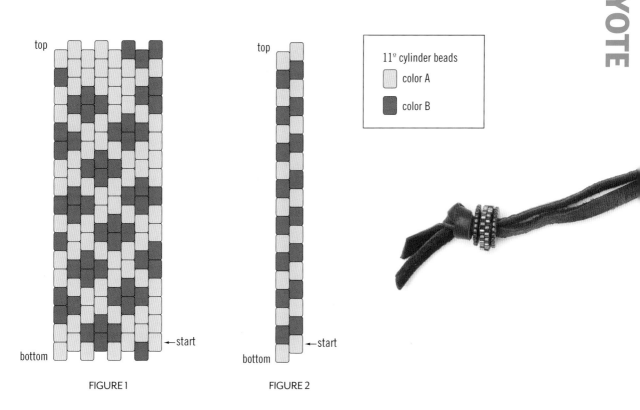

top

top

11° cylinder beads

color A

color B

←start

←start

bottom

bottom

FIGURE 1

FIGURE 2

PEYOTE CHANNEL CHARM

1 On 1 yd. (.9 m) of thread, attach a stop bead, leaving a 6-in. (15 cm) tail. Starting at the lower-right corner of **figure 1**, pick up 11° cylinder beads for rows 1 and 2: one A, one B, two As, one B, three As.

2 Following figure 1, work in flat even-count peyote stitch using the appropriate color cylinders. Remove the stop bead, and end the tail, but do not end the working thread.

3 Wrap the peyote band around the center of a medium channel bead, and zip up the ends. Retrace the thread path, and end the working thread.

4 On a head pin, string a 6 mm pearl, the medium channel bead, and a 6 mm pearl. Make a wrapped loop.

PEYOTE CHANNEL BEAD

1 On 24 in. (61 cm) of thread, attach a stop bead, leaving a 6-in. (15 cm) tail. Starting at the lower-right corner of **figure 2**, pick up two As for rows 1 and 2.

2 Following figure 2, work in flat even-count peyote stitch using the appropriate color cylinders. Remove the stop bead, and end the tail, but do not end the working thread.

3 Wrap the peyote band around the center of a small channel bead, and zip up the ends. Retrace the thread path, and end the working thread.

ASSEMBLY

1 Open a 9 mm jump ring, and attach the peyote channel charm to one loop of the oval connector, positioning the charm so it hangs within the oval.

2 Open the loop of an eye pin, and attach the heart charm.

3 On the same eye pin, string a 15 mm square gemstone and a 15 x 30 mm rectangle gemstone. Make the first half of a wrapped loop, leaving approximately 6 mm between the top bead and the loop. Attach the other loop of the oval connector, and complete the wraps.

4 Attach the following jump rings around the eye pin between the top bead and the wrapped loop: one 9 mm, three 11.3 mm, and one 9 mm.

5 Fold the deerskin lace in half, and pull the folded end through the oval connector from front to back. Pull the ends of the lace through the fold, placing one on either side of the peyote channel charm.

6 Over both ends of the lace, string the peyote channel bead. Slide the bead down the lace several inches, and tie an overhand knot with both ends of the lace. Slide the bead toward the knot or away from it to adjust the length of the necklace.

Heart's desire bracelet

Capture coveted crystals at the center of this pattern traced with a subtle heart motif.

designed by Lorraine Coetzee

BASE

You will end and add thread multiple times as you stitch the base. Always add a new thread so that you can stitch even-numbered rows from left to right and odd-numbered rows from right to left. This will ensure proper tension along the edges.

1 On a comfortable length of thread, attach a stop bead, leaving a 30-in. (76 cm) tail. Starting at the top-left corner of the top end section of **figure 1**, pick up the 11⁰ cylinder beads outlined in orange: one B, four Cs, two As, two Ds, two As, one B, three Cs, one B, two As, two Ds, two As, four Cs,

one B. These beads will shift to form rows 1 and 2 of the end section as the next row is added. The tapered end rows will be added later.

2 Following the pattern in **figure 1**, work rows 3–21 in odd-count peyote stitch.

note At the end of row 3, work a figure-8 turn to get ready for the next row. For all other odd-numbered rows, you may make the turn by picking up the last bead of the row, sewing under the nearest thread bridge along the edge, and sewing back through the last bead added.

FIGURE 1

Start

End section

Side strips

End section

MATERIALS

bracelet 7½ in. (19.1 cm)

- **11** 6 x 8 mm faceted crystal rondelles (green iris)
- **3 g** 8º cylinder beads (Miyuki DBL0023, metallic smoky gold iris)
- **3 g** 11º seed beads (Toho 377, teal-lined metallic light sapphire)
- 11º cylinder beads
  - **4 g** color A (Miyuki DB455, nickel finish light purple)
  - **2 g** color B (Miyuki DB1831, Duracoat galvanized silver)
  - **6 g** color C (Miyuki DB0351, matte white)
  - **1 g** color D (Miyuki DB1847, Duracoat galvanized sea foam)
  - **1 g** color E (Miyuki DB0040, metallic copper)
- nylon beading thread
- beading needles, #10 or #12

TECHNIQUES

- beading fundamentals: attaching a stop bead, ending and adding thread, square knot (p. 20)
- peyote stitch: flat odd-count, flat even-count, decreasing at the end of a row, tubular, zipping up (p. 24)

11º cylinder beads

- color A
- color B
- color C
- color D
- color E

a

Row 22

b

c

d

FIGURE 2

3 Work the first six stitches of row 22 (**figure 2, a–b**). Sew through the next two beads as shown (**b–c**), and work the last six stitches of the row (**c–d**). This row is outlined in pink in **figure 1**. Set this section aside but don't end the threads.

4 Repeat steps 1–3 to make the other end section.

5 On a comfortable length of thread, attach a stop bead, leaving a 6-in. (15 cm) tail. Starting at the top-left corner of the left-hand side strip of **figure 1**, pick up the 11º cylinder beads outlined in green: one C, two As, one B, three As, one B, two As, one C. These beads will shift to form rows 1 and 2 of the side strip as the next row is added. Work the remaining rows to create the left side of the split band. End the threads, and set this strip aside.

FIGURE 3

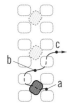

FIGURE 4

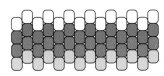

FIGURE 5

6 Repeat step 5 to work the other side strip.

7 Align the side strips between the end sections, and using the working threads from the end sections, zip all the segments together.

8 Working with the tail remaining from an end section, sew through the beadwork so the thread exits the same bead it was exiting from, but in the opposite direction. Work the first three rows of the tapered end in odd-count peyote.

9 To work a decrease, sew under the nearest thread bridge along the edge, and continue back through the last two beads you just sewed through (**figure 3**).

10 Work the remaining rows of the tapered end, decreasing at the end of each row until you have just one bead in the final row. End the working thread.

11 Repeat steps 8–10 at the other end of the band, and end the tail.

CENTER RONDELLES

Add a comfortable length of thread to the beadwork, sew toward the split, and exit the cylinder bead indicated by the top red line in figure 1. Pick up a 6 x 8 mm rondelle, and sew through the corresponding cylinder on the other side of the split. Retrace the thread path through the rondelle, and sew through the beadwork to exit the cylinder indicated by the second red line in **figure 1**. Continue adding rondelles in this manner for the length of the bracelet, and end the thread.

EDGING

1 Add a comfortable length of thread to the base, and exit the first cylinder along one straight edge. Rotate your work so that this edge is at the top.

2 Pick up an 8° cylinder bead and three 11° seed beads, sew back through the 8°, continue down through the next cylinder along the edge, and sew up through the following cylinder along the edge.

3 Repeat step 2 for the entire edge. Sew through the beadwork to exit the first cylinder along the other straight edge, and repeat step 2 for this edge.

TOGGLE RING

1 On 1½ yd. (1.4 m) of thread, pick up 26 Cs. Tie them into a ring with a square knot, leaving a 6-in. (15 cm) tail. Sew through the first few Cs in the ring.

2 Work a round of tubular peyote stitch using one C per stitch. Work another round using two Cs per stitch.

3 Sew through the beadwork to exit a C in round 1, and work two rounds using one E per stitch.

4 Work a round using two Cs per stitch, and step up through the first C added in this round. Pinch the beadwork so that the rounds with two Cs per stitch are aligned.

5 Pick up an E, and sew through the second C in the corresponding pair of the opposite round (**figure 4, a–b**). Continue through the first C in the next pair of the original round (**b–c**). Repeat this stitch 12 times to zip up the outside of the toggle ring, and exit the first E added in this round.

6 Pick up an 8°, three 11°s, and an 8°, and sew through the next E in the round. Repeat this stitch 12 times to complete the round, and step up through the first 8° and two 11°s added in this round.

7 To connect the toggle ring to the base, sew through the single A at one tip of the base, and sew through the 11° in the toggle ring again. Retrace the thread path several times, and end the working thread and tail.

TOGGLE BAR

1 On 1 yd. (.9 m) of thread, attach a stop bead, leaving a 6-in. (15 cm) tail. Following the pattern in **figure 5**, work the toggle bar in even-count peyote stitch. Zip up the edges to form the bar.

2 Exit a cylinder at the center of the bar, sew through the single A at the remaining tip of the base, and sew through the cylinder in the toggle bar again. Retrace the thread path several times, and end the working thread. Remove the stop bead from the tail, and end the tail.

Petite presentation

Netted beaded beads highlighted by gemstones act as an understated focal point in this classic necklace. Choose your favorite stones and colors for an everyday accessory you will love to wear.

designed by Lesley Weiss

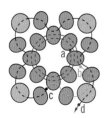

FIGURE 1

BEADED BEADS

1 On 24 in. (61 cm) of thread, pick up eight 11º seed beads, leaving a 6-in. (15 cm) tail. Sew through all the 11ºs again to form a ring, then continue through the first 11º picked up (**figure 1, a–b**).

2 Pick up an 11º, a 3 mm round bead, and an 11º, skip the next 11º in the ring, and sew through the following 11º (**b–c**). Repeat around the ring, and step up through the first 11º and 3 mm added in this round (**c–d**).

MATERIALS
necklace 18¼ in. (46.4 cm)
- **48** 5 x 7 mm gemstone rondelles
- 16-in. (41 cm) strand 3 mm round gemstones
- **5 g** 11º seed beads
- clasp
- **2** crimp beads
- flexible beading wire, .014
- WildFire beading thread
- beading needles, #13
- crimping pliers
- wire cutters

TECHNIQUES
- beading fundamentals: attaching a stop bead, ending and adding thread, square knot, crimping (p. 20)
- netting (p. 34)

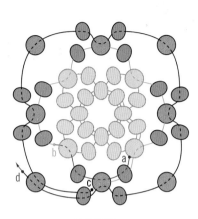

FIGURE 2

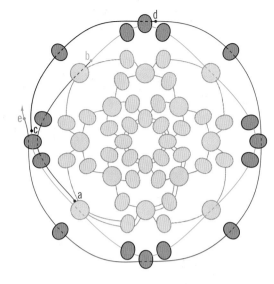

FIGURE 3

3 Pick up an 11º, a 3 mm, and an 11º, and sew through the next 3 mm in the previous round (**figure 2, a–b**). Repeat around the ring, and step up through the first 11º and 3 mm added in this round (**b–c**).

4 Repeat step 3 to add another round of netting (**c–d**). The beadwork will begin to form a cup shape.

5 Pick up three 11ºs, and sew through the next 3 mm in the previous round (**figure 3, a–b**). Repeat around, and step up through the first two 11ºs added in this round (**b–c**).

6 Pick up an 11º, and sew through the middle 11º in the next stitch in the previous round (**c–d**). Repeat around (**d–e**), and sew through the eight 11ºs of the final round again.

7 Retrace the thread paths to reinforce the bead. End the thread. Thread a needle on the tail, and repeat.

8 Repeat steps 1–7 to make a total of nine beaded beads.

ASSEMBLY

1 Cut a 24-in. (61 cm) piece of beading wire, and center an 11º, a beaded bead, and an 11º.

2 On each end, string a 5 x 7 mm rondelle, an 11º, a beaded bead, and an 11º. Repeat until all nine beaded beads have been strung.

3 On each end, string a 5 x 7 mm rondelle and a 3 mm. Repeat until the necklace has 20 3 mms on each end.

4 On each end, string a crimp bead and half of the clasp. Go back through each crimp bead, and crimp it. Trim the wire tails.

TIP Gemstones sometimes have small holes that are hard to sew through multiple times. If you have trouble passing your needle through a bead on the first attempt, you may want to discard the bead and use another since it will likely break the next time you try to sew through it.

Diamonds and pearls

Diamond-shaped embellishments frame pearl insets along the length of this pretty bracelet. With the range of color choices available in crystals and pearls, there's no end to the color combinations you can stitch.

designed by Janice Chatham

MATERIALS

bracelet 6 in. (15 cm)
- **8** 4 mm crystal pearls
- **132** 3 mm bicone crystals
- **4 g** 15º seed beads
- clasp
- **2** 4–5 mm jump rings
- Fireline 6 lb. test
- beading needles, #12
- **2** pairs of pliers

TECHNIQUES
- beading fundamentals: attaching a stop bead, ending and adding thread, square knot, crimping (p. 20)
- netting (p. 34)

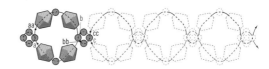

FIGURE 1

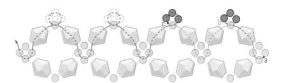

FIGURE 2

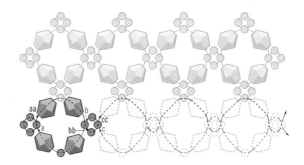

FIGURE 3

BAND ONE

1 Thread a needle on each end of 2 yd. (1.8 m) of Fireline, and center four 15º seed beads. Cross one needle through an end 15º, and pull the beads into a ring.

2 With one needle, pick up a 3 mm bicone crystal, a 15º, a 3 mm, and a 15º. With the other needle, pick up a 3 mm, a 15º, and a 3 mm, and cross through the last 15º picked up with the first needle (**figure 1, a–b and aa–bb**).

3 With one needle, pick up two 15ºs. With the other needle, pick up one 15º, and cross through the second 15º picked up with the first needle (**b–c and bb–cc**).

4 Repeat steps 2 and 3 until you have a total of 16 clusters of 3 mms. With one needle, sew through the next two 15ºs, 3 mm, and 15º (**figure 2, a–b**).

5 Pick up three 15ºs, sew through the 15º your thread just exited, and continue through the next 3 mm, three 15ºs, 3 mm, and 15º (**b–c**).

6 Repeat step 5 for the length of the band.

7 Repeat steps 5 and 6 to add picots to the other edge. End the threads.

BAND TWO

1 On 3 yd. (2.7 m) of Fireline, repeat step 1 of "Band one."

2 With one needle, pick up a 3 mm, a 15º, a 3 mm, and a 15º. With the other needle, pick up a 3 mm, and sew through the middle 15º in the first picot of band one. Pick up a 3 mm, and cross through the last 15º picked up with the first needle (**figure 3, a–b and aa–bb**).

3 With one needle, pick up two 15ºs. With the other needle, pick up a 15º, and cross through the second 15º picked up with the first needle (**b–c and bb–cc**).

4 Repeat steps 2 and 3 for the length of band one.

5 Sew through the beadwork to exit the first 15º on the new edge, and repeat step 5 of "Band one" to add picots along the other edge.

END LOOPS AND EMBELLISHMENT

1 With the working thread, sew through the beadwork to exit at **figure 4, point a**. Pick up a 3 mm, a 15º, and a 3 mm, and sew through the end loop on the other band as shown (**a–b**). Sew back through the second 3 mm and the 15º, and pick up five 15ºs. Sew through the 15º again, and continue through the next 3 mm and three 15ºs of the

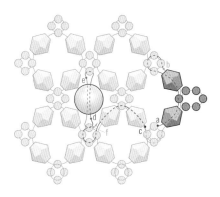

FIGURE 4

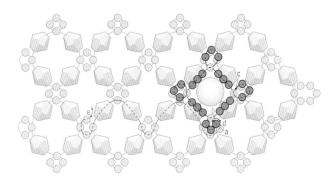

FIGURE 5

 TIPS **If needed, lengthen the bracelet in one of two ways:**
- **Add more jump rings between the bands and the clasp.**
- **Stitch two more clusters of 3 mms on each band for an additional ¾ in. (1.9 cm) in length.**

end loop on the first band (**b–c**). Sew through the next 3 mm, 15⁰, 3 mm, and four 15⁰s (**c–d**).
2 Pick up a 4 mm pearl, and sew through the corresponding 15⁰ on the other band (**d–e**). Sew back through the 4 mm and the 15⁰ your thread exited at the start of this step (**e–f**).
3 Pick up three 15⁰s, and sew through the 15⁰ your thread just exited (**figure 5, a–b**). Pick up three 15⁰s, and sew through the 15⁰ to the right of the 4 mm (**b–c**). Continue adding picots and three-bead connectors around the 4 mm until you sew through the 15⁰ your thread exited at the start of this step (**c–d**).
4 Sew through the next two clusters of 3 mms, and exit the center 15⁰ of the following group of 15⁰s (**d–e**).

5 Repeat steps 2–4 across the band to add an embellished pearl in the center of every other group of clusters.
6 Add a loop at the other end of the bands, as in step 1. End the threads.
7 Open a jump ring, attach an end loop and one half of the clasp, and close the jump ring. Repeat on the other end.

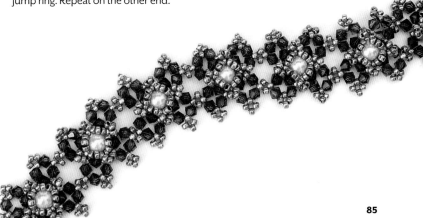

Peanut party bracelet

Brick stitch a diamond pattern of peanut beads, and add an easy embellishment on top for a stunning bracelet.

designed by Jimmie Boatright

mix it up
ALSO FEATURING
LADDER STITCH

BASE

1 On a comfortable length of thread and leaving a 6-in. (15 cm) tail, work a 10-bead ladder using three color A peanut beads, four color B peanut beads, and three As **(figure 1, a–b)**. This will be row 1 of the base. End and add thread throughout the pattern as needed.

2 Work row 2 in brick stitch as follows, noting the different terms for each kind of stitch:

Decrease start stitch: Pick up two As, sew under the second-to-last thread bridge in the previous row, and sew back up through the last A just added. Sew through both beads to align them (not shown in the figure for clarity), and exit the last A **(b–c)**.

Regular stitch: Pick up a B, sew under the next thread bridge in the previous row, and sew back up through the B just added. Work four more regular stitches using Bs, and two using As **(c–d)**.

3 Continue to work in rows as follows:

Row 3: Decrease start stitch using an A and a B; five regular stitches using Bs; one regular stitch using an A **(d–e)**.

Row 4: Decrease start stitch using two Bs; five regular stitches using Bs **(e–f)**.

Row 5: Increase start stitch: Pick up two Bs, sew under the last thread bridge in the previous row, and sew back up through the last B just added **(f–g)**; five regular stitches using Bs; increase end stitch: pick up a B, sew under the same thread bridge as in the previous stitch, and sew back up through the B just added **(g–h)**.

Row 6: Increase start stitch using two Bs; six regular stitches using Bs; one increase end stitch using a B **(h–i)**.

Row 7: Increase start stitch using two Bs; seven regular stitches using Bs; one increase end stitch using a B **(i–j)**.

Row 8: Increase start stitch using two Bs; eight regular stitches using Bs; one increase end stitch using a B **(j–k)**.

Row 9: Decrease start stitch using two Bs; eight regular stitches using Bs **(k–l)**.

Row 10: Decrease start stitch using two Bs; seven regular stitches using Bs **(l–m)**.

Row 11: Decrease start stitch using two Bs; six regular stitches using Bs **(m–n)**.

Row 12: Decrease start stitch using two Bs; five regular stitches using Bs **(n–o)**.

Row 13: Increase start stitch using an A and a B; five regular stitches using Bs; one increase end stitch using an A **(o–p)**.

Row 14: Increase start stitch using two As; five regular stitches using Bs and one using an A; one increase end stitch using an A **(p–q)**.

Row 15: Increase start stitch using two As; one regular stitch using an A, four using Bs, and two using As; one increase end stitch using an A **(q–r)**.

Row 16: Increase start stitch using two As; two regular stitches using As, three using Bs, and three using As; one increase end stitch using an A **(r–s)**.

Row 17: Increase start stitch using two As; three regular stitches using As, two using Bs, and four using As; one increase end stitch using an A **(s–t)**.

Row 18: Increase start stitch using two As; four regular stitches using As, one using a B, and five using As; one increase end stitch using an A **(t–u)**.

Row 19: Increase start stitch using two As; eleven regular stitches using As; one increase end stitch using an A **(u–v)**.

Row 20: Decrease start stitch using two As; four regular stitches using As, one using a B, and six using As **(v–w)**.

Row 21: Decrease start stitch using two As; three regular stitches using As, two using Bs, and five using As **(w–x)**.

Row 22: Decrease start stitch using two As; two regular stitches using As, three using Bs, and four using As **(x–y)**.

FIGURE 1

Legend:

- 2 x 4 mm peanut bead, color A (top view)
- 2 x 4 mm peanut bead, color B (top view)
- 11° seed bead
- 4 mm fire-polished bead
- 4 mm round bead

MATERIALS

orange bracelet 1⅜ x 7 in. (3.5 x 18 cm)

- **28** 4 mm fire-polished beads (opaque dark red)
- **28** 4 mm round druk beads (opaque green luster)
- 2 x 4 mm peanut beads
  - **6 g** color A (opaque moss green luster)
  - **6 g** color B (opaque coral luster)
- **1 g** 11° seed bead (Toho 262, crystal gold-lined)
- **1** 5-strand tube clasp
- nylon beading thread, size D
- beading needles, #11 or #12

TECHNIQUES

- beading fundamentals: attaching a stop bead, ending and adding thread, square knot, crimping (p. 20)
- herringbone stitch: tubular (p. 42)
- ladder stitch: making a ladder, forming a ring (p. 36)

Row 23: Decrease start stitch using two As; one regular stitch using an A, four using Bs, and three using As (**y–z**).

Row 24: Decrease start stitch using two As; five regular stitches using Bs, and two using As (**z–aa**).

Row 25: Decrease start stitch using an A and a B; five regular stitches using Bs; one regular stitch using an A (**aa–bb**).

Row 26: Decrease start stitch using two Bs; five regular stitches using Bs (**bb–cc**).

4 Repeat rows 13–26 (**cc–dd**).

5 Repeat rows 5–26 and then rows 13–26. Finish the base by working rows 5–15 for a 7 in. (18 cm) bracelet. To make the pattern longer, continue working the pattern on both ends. To use a 5-strand clasp, be sure to end with 10 beads in the last row.

CLASP

Pick up an A and an 11º seed bead, sew back through the A just added, and continue down through the end loop of the clasp (**figure 2, a–b**). Pick up an A and an 11º, sew back through the A

just added, and continue up through the same clasp loop, the next end peanut bead, and the following peanut bead (**b–c**). Repeat these stitches for the remainder of the clasp loops, except use Bs instead of As for the center loop (**c–d**).

EMBELLISHMENT RING

1 On 2 ft. (61 cm) of thread, work in ladder stitch using two As, two Bs, two As, and two Bs, and join them into a ring (**figure 3**).

2 Working in herringbone stitch, pick up two Bs, sew down through the adjacent B, and continue up through the next A (**figure 4, a–b**). Pick up two As, sew down through the adjacent A, and continue up through the next B (**b–c**). Repeat these stitches once more, and sew through the first B added in this round (**c–d**).

3 Pick up a 4 mm fire-polished bead, and sew down through the adjacent B (**d–e**). Pick up a 4 mm round bead, and sew up through the next A (**e–f**). Repeat these stitches three times to

complete the round, and sew through the first fire-polished bead added (**f–g**).

4 Pick up an 11º, and sew through the next round bead (**g–h**). Pick up an 11º, and sew through the following fire-polished bead (**h–i**). Repeat these stitches three times to complete the round (**i–j**), and retrace the thread path. End the tail, but not the working thread.

5 Repeat steps 1–4 to make six more embellishment rings.

6 Position a ring on the base in the center of a diamond, with the fire-polished beads sitting horizontally and vertically on the base. Sew through an adjacent peanut directly below the bead your thread is exiting, and continue through the nearest bead in the ring. Repeat this stitch around the ring to attach it to the base, and end the thread. Repeat to add the remaining embellishment rings to the centers of the diamonds.

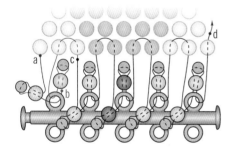

FIGURE 2

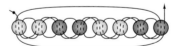

FIGURE 3

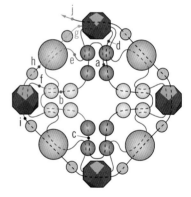

FIGURE 4

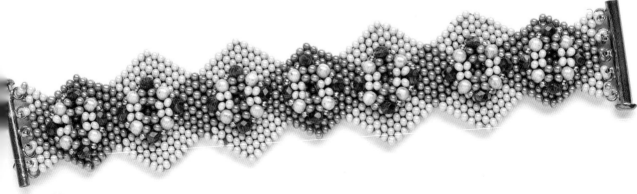

Blooming petals bracelet

Stitch a playful bracelet with a mixture of vibrant colors that feature petal-like Pip beads sprouting from the center.

designed by Cassie Donlen

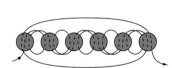

mix it up
ALSO FEATURING
LADDER STITCH

BASE

1 On a comfortable length of thread, using a #12 needle and leaving an 8-in. (20 cm) tail, work in ladder stitch using color A 11º seed beads to make a six-bead ladder. Sew through the first and last beads to form the ladder into a ring **(figure 1)**.

2 Pick up two As, sew down through the next A in the ladder, and continue up through the following A **(figure 2, a–b)**. Repeat this stitch twice to complete the round, and step up through the first A added in this round **(b–c)**.

3 To make a 7¾-in. (19.7 cm) bracelet, continue working in tubular herringbone stitch using the following color pattern: Work a round using color B 11º seed beads, a round using color C

11º seed beads, a round using color D 11º seed beads, a round using Cs, and a round using Bs.

4 Work 15 rounds using As. Continue working rounds in the following color pattern: B, C, D, Pip beads (pick up the Pip beads in the same manner as the 11ºs), D, C, B.

note To adjust the bracelet length, work more or fewer rounds in each section of As, being sure to work the same number of rounds in each A section. Adding or omitting one round in each A section equals a total of about ¼ in. (6 mm).

5 Repeat step 4 twice, work 15 rounds using As, repeat step 3 once, and then work two rounds using As.

FIGURE 1

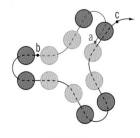

FIGURE 2

MATERIALS

bracelet 9 in. (23 cm)

- **18** 7 x 5 mm Pip beads (alabaster pastel emerald)
- **1 g** 3.4 mm drop beads (violet gold luster)
- **14** 3 mm bicone crystals (Swarovski, jet AB2X)
- **42** 2 mm pearls (Czech, eggplant)
- 11º seed beads
  - **8 g** color A (pink-lined amethyst AB)
  - **1 g** color B (galvanized saffron)
  - **1 g** color C (silver-lined matte blue)
  - **1 g** color D (dark chocolate brown)
- **1 g** 15º seed beads (metallic orange)
- toggle clasp
- Fireline, 6 lb. test
- beading needles, #12 and #13

TECHNIQUES

- beading fundamentals: ending and adding thread (p. 20)
- ladder stitch: making a ladder, forming a ring (p. 36)
- herringbone stitch: tubular (p. 42)

CLASP

1 Secure the loose stacks in the last two rounds of the base: Without adding any new beads and working in the opposite direction, sew down through the two end As in the previous stack (**photo**), and continue up through the two As in the following stack. Repeat this stitch twice to complete the round.

2 With the working thread, pick up six As and the loop of the toggle ring. Skip the next two As in the end round of the base, and sew down through the following two As in the next stack. Retrace the thread path to reinforce the connection, and end the working thread.

3 With the tail, repeat step 2 to add the toggle bar to the other end.

SLIDER BEADS

1 On 1 yd. (.9 m) of thread and using a #13 needle, pick up four 2 mm pearls, and tie a square knot to form the pearls into a ring, leaving a 6-in. (15 cm) tail. Sew through the first three beads again (**figure 3, a–b**). Picking up three pearls per stitch, work five more right-angle weave (RAW) stitches (**b–c**).

2 Wrap the strip around the base between two sections of Pip beads. Form the strip into a ring: Pick up a pearl, and sew through the end pearl in the first stitch. Pick up a pearl and sew through

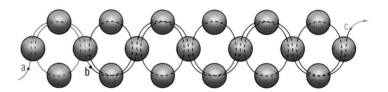

FIGURE 3

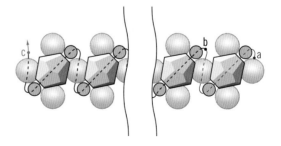

FIGURE 4

the end pearl in the last stitch. Retrace the thread path to reinforce the join.

3 Pick up a 15º seed bead, a 3 mm crystal, and a 15º. Cross the RAW stitch diagonally, and sew through the next corresponding pearl, going in the same direction (**figure 4, a–b**). Repeat this stitch six times to complete the round (**b–c**).

4 Sew through the edge pearl in the next RAW stitch (**figure 5, a–b**). Pick up a drop bead, and sew through the edge pearl in the following RAW stitch (**b–c**). Repeat this stitch six times to complete the round (**c–d**).

5 Sew through the beadwork to exit a pearl on the other edge, and work as in step 4 to add a total of seven drops on this edge of the slider bead. End the working thread and tail.

6 Repeat steps 1–5 to add a second slider bead to the corresponding section on the base.

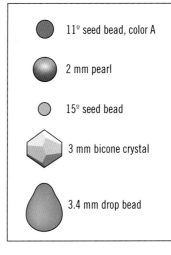

●	11º seed bead, color A
●	2 mm pearl
○	15º seed bead
◆	3 mm bicone crystal
◗	3.4 mm drop bead

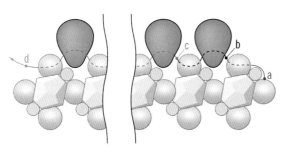

FIGURE 5

Tila sunrise necklace

Greet the new day with a rivoli enclosed in a basket of Tila beads, crystals, and other accents.

designed by Cary Borelli

MATERIALS
necklace 19 in. (48 cm)
- **1** 27 mm rivoli (Swarovski, purple haze)
- **20** 5 x 5 mm Tila beads (Miyuki, transparent oyster luster)
- **16** 6 mm round beads (opaque amethyst luster)
- **40** 4 mm fire-polishedbeads (polychrome copper rose)
- **40** 3 mm round beads (luster transparent amethyst)
- **64** 3 mm bicone crystals (Swarovski, lilac shadow)
- **8** 8º seed beads (Toho 993, gold-lined black diamond)
- **10 g** 11º seed beads (Toho 1700, gilded marble white)
- **1 g** 15º seed beads (Miyuki 312, amethyst gold luster)
- toggle clasp (brass)
- **2** 6 mm filigree bead caps (brass)
- Fireline, 8 lb. test
- beading needles, #11

TECHNIQUES
- beading fundamentals: ending and adding thread, square knot (p. 20)
- herringbone stitch: tubular (p. 42)
- ladder stitch: making a ladder, forming a ring (p. 36)

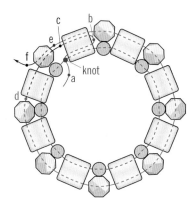

FIGURE 1

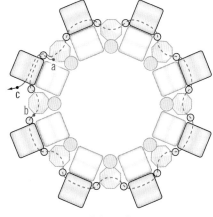

FIGURE 2

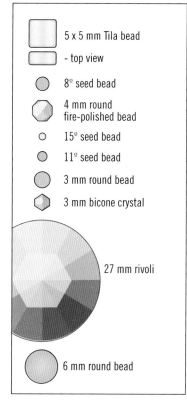

5 x 5 mm Tila bead

- top view

8º seed bead

4 mm round
fire-polished bead

15º seed bead

11º seed bead

3 mm round bead

3 mm bicone crystal

27 mm rivoli

6 mm round bead

PENDANT

1 On 2 yd. (1.8 m) of thread, pick up a repeating pattern of a Tila bead and an 8º seed bead eight times. Tie the beads into a ring with a square knot, leaving a 6-in. (15 cm) tail. Continue through the first Tila (**figure 1, a–b**), and sew through the open hole of the same Tila (**b–c**).

2 Pick up a 4 mm fire-polished bead, and sew through the open hole of the next Tila (**c–d**). Repeat this stitch seven

times to complete the round (**d–e**), and sew through the first 4 mm added in this round (**e–f**).

3 Pick up a 15º seed bead, a Tila, and a 15º, and sew through the next 4 mm (**figure 2, a–b**). Pull the thread tight, and "flip up" the Tila to start creating a basket shape. Repeat this stitch seven times to complete the round, and sew through the first 15º and Tila added in this round (**b–c**).

FIGURE 3

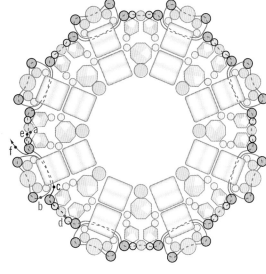

FIGURE 4

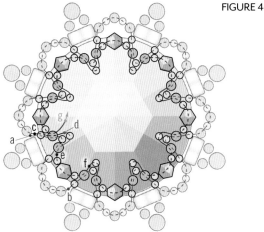

FIGURE 5

4 Pick up a 15º, an 11º seed bead, a 3 mm round bead, an 11º, and a 15º. Sew through the same hole of the Tila again, going in the same direction, to form a loop of beads around the Tila on the outside of the basket (**figure 3, a–b**). In figures 3 and 4, these beads are shown above the Tila for visibility.

5 Pick up a 15º, a 3 mm bicone crystal, an 11º, a 3 mm crystal, and a 15º, and sew through the next Tila (**b–c**).

6 Repeat steps 4–5 seven times to complete the round (**c–d**), and sew through the first 15º, 3 mm crystal, and 11º added in this round (**d–e**).

7 Pick up a 15º and an 11º, and sew through the open hole of the next Tila (**figure 4, a–b**).

8 Pick up an 11º, sew back through the 3 mm round in the loop around this Tila, pick up an 11º, and sew through the Tila again (**b–c**).

9 Pick up an 11º and a 15º, and sew through the next 11º (**c–d**).

10 Repeat steps 7–9 seven times to complete the round (**d–e**), and sew through the first 15º and 11º added in this round (**e–f**). Place the 27 mm rivoli faceup in the basket.

11 Pick up a 15º, an 11º, a 15º, an 11º, and a 15º. Skip the next Tila and the beads on the outside of the basket, and sew through the following five seed beads (**figure 5, a–b**). Repeat this stitch seven times to complete the round (**b–c**), and sew through the first 15º and 11º added in this round (**c–d**).

12 Pick up a 15º, skip the next 15º, and sew through the following 11º (**d–e**).

13 Pick up a 15º, a 3 mm crystal, and a 15º, skip the next seven seed beads, and sew through the following 11º (**e–f**).

14 Repeat steps 12–13 seven times to complete the round (**f–g**). Retrace the thread path of this round, and end the working thread and tail.

FIGURE 6

FIGURE 7

FIGURE 8

FIGURE 9

FIGURE 10

FIGURE 11

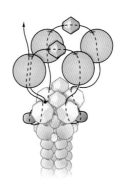

FIGURE 12

BEADED ROPES

1 On a comfortable length of thread and leaving a 12-in. (30 cm) tail, work a four-bead ladder using 11ºs (**figure 6**). Form the ladder into a ring.

2 Pick up two 11ºs, sew down through the next 11º in the ladder (**figure 7, a–b**), and continue up through the following 11º (**b–c**). Work a second herringbone stitch, and sew through the first 11º added in this round (**figure 8**).

3 Continue working in tubular herringbone stitch using 11ºs for a total of 11 rounds, including the ladder ring.

4 Continue working rounds of herringbone as follows:

Round 12: Two herringbone stitches, each with an 11º, a 15º, and an 11º. Step up through the first 11º added in this round (**figure 9**).

note You will always step up through the first bead added in each round no matter how many beads are added in the herringbone stitches.

Round 13: Two stitches, each with a 3 mm round, an 11º, and a 3 mm round (**figure 10**).

Round 14: Work a herringbone stitch with a 4 mm, a 3 mm crystal, and a 4 mm (**figure 11, a–b**). Add a 15º between the stitches (**b–c**). Work another herringbone stitch with the same beads as before, and add a 15º between the stitches (**c–d**).

Round 15: Two stitches, each with a 6 mm round bead, a 3 mm crystal, and a 6 mm, adding an 11º between the stitches (**figure 12**).

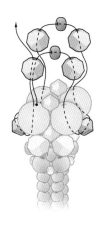

FIGURE 13

FIGURE 14

FIGURE 15

FIGURE 16

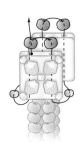

FIGURE 17

FIGURE 18

Round 16: Two stitches, each with a 4 mm, an 11º and a 4 mm, adding a 3 mm crystal between the stitches (**figure 13**).

Round 17: Two stitches, each with a 3 mm round, a 15º, and a 3 mm round, adding a 3 mm crystal between the stitches (**figure 14**).

Round 18: Two stitches, each with two 11ºs, adding an 11º between the stitches.

Round 19: Two stitches, each with two 11ºs, adding a 15º between the stitches.

5 Continue working in tubular herringbone stitch using 11ºs (without adding any beads between stitches) for a total of 12 rounds, including rounds 18 and 19. End and add thread as needed.

6 For round 30, work two stitches each with a Tila, sewing through both holes of the Tila as if they were two beads. Step up through the first hole of the first Tila added in this round (**figure 15**).

7 Pick up a 15º, a 3 mm crystal, a 15º, a 3 mm crystal, and a 15º. Cross the Tila diagonally, and sew up through the other hole of the same Tila (**figure 16, a–b**). Pick up a 15º and a 3 mm crystal, and sew through the 15º at the center of the diagonal line of beads. Pick up a 3 mm crystal and a 15º, and sew up through the first hole of the Tila (**b–c**).

8 For round 31, work two stitches with two 11ºs each, sewing through both holes of the Tilas as if they were two beads and adding a 15º between stitches (**figure 17**).

9 For round 32, work two stitches with 11ºs, adding a 15º between the stitches (**figure 18**).

10 Continue working in tubular herringbone stitch using 11ºs (without adding any beads between stitches) for a total of 11 rounds, including rounds 31 and 32.

11 Repeat rounds 12–19.

12 Continue working in tubular herringbone stitch using 11ºs (without adding any beads between stitches) until your rope reaches about half your desired necklace length. Do not end the working thread or tail.

13 Repeat steps 1–12 to make another beaded rope.

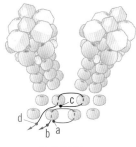

FIGURE 19

FIGURE 20

FIGURE 21

FIGURE 22

ROPE ATTACHMENTS

1 Align the starting ends of the ropes, making sure the crystal embellishments on the Tilas are facing forward.
2 With the tail from one rope, work a ladder stitch thread path through the adjacent 11⁰s at the front of the ladder rings (**figure 19, a–b**). Retrace the thread path several times, and end the tail. Repeat with the other tail for the two 11⁰s at the back of the join (**c–d**), but do not end the tail.
3 Position the pendant under the joined ropes, aligning one of the Tilas of the basket with the join. The ropes will be attached to the beads on the outside of this Tila.

4 Sew through the nearest back 11⁰ on the outside of the Tila, the 3 mm round at the center of the Tila, and the other back 11⁰ on the outside of the Tila. Continue through the corresponding 11⁰ at the back of the other rope (**figure 20**).
5 Sew down through the 11⁰ at the front of the join. Pick up an 11⁰, sew through the 3 mm round at the center of the Tila, pick up an 11⁰, and sew through the other 11⁰ at the front of the join (**figure 21**). Retrace the thread path of the pendant connections, and end the tail.

CLASP

With the working thread from either rope, pick up a bead cap, an 11⁰, three 15⁰s, half of the clasp, and three 15⁰s. Sew back through the 11⁰ and bead cap, and sew through the opposite 11⁰ in the last round (**figure 22**). Retrace the thread path, and end the thread. Repeat with the working thread from the other rope.

Extravaganza bracelet

Stitch a colorful base of fire-polished beads, and then strategically adorn it with crystals, magatamas, and seed beads for an exquisite look.

designed by Cassie Donlen

⬡	4 mm fire-polished bead, color A
⬢	4 mm fire-polished bead, color B
⬡	4 mm fire-polished bead, color C
●	2 mm fire-polished bead
🝆	3 mm magatama bead
●	15º seed bead
⬡	4 mm bicone crystal

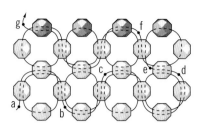

FIGURE 1

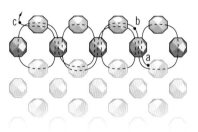

FIGURE 2

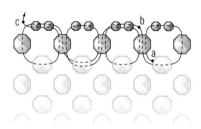

FIGURE 3

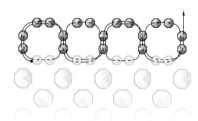

FIGURE 4

MATERIALS

bracelet 7½ in. (19.1 cm)

- · 4 mm fire-polished beads
  - **60** color A (orchid aqua polychrome)
  - **72** color B (copper rose polychrome)
  - **76** color C (azurite halo)
- · **80** 4 mm bicone crystals
  (Swarovski, jet AB2X)
- · **7 g** 3 mm magatamas
  (Toho 702, dark copper)
- · **78** 2 mm fire-polished beads
  (orchid mirror)
- · **2 g** 15º seed beads
  (Toho 460G, steel blue metallic)
- · **1** 5-strand tube clasp
- · Fireline, 6 lb. test
- · beading needles, #11 or #12

TECHNIQUES

- · beading fundamentals: ending and
  adding thread (p. 20)
- · right-angle weave: flat strip,
  adding rows (p. 46)

BASE

1 On a comfortable length of thread, pick up four color A 4 mm fire-polished beads, and sew through the beads again to form a ring, leaving a 6-in. (15 cm) tail. Continue through the first three As **(figure 1, a–b)**. This forms the first stitch.
2 Working in right-angle weave (RAW), pick up three As, and sew through the A your thread exited at the start of this step. Continue through the first two As just added **(b–c)**, and tighten. Continue working in RAW for a total of four stitches to form the first row **(c–d)**, and then sew through the top edge bead of the last stitch **(d–e)** to get into position to start row 2.
3 Continue working in RAW using fire-polished beads:
Row 2: Pick up an A, a color B 4 mm fire-polished bead, and an A for the first stitch **(e–f)**. Continue working in RAW following the established color pattern to complete the row **(f–g)**.
Row 3: Work a row using Bs.

Row 4: Work the first stitch with a B, a color C fire-polished bead, and a B **(figure 2, a–b)**. Continue working in RAW following the established color pattern to complete the row **(b–c)**.
Row 5: Work a row using Cs.
Row 6: Work the first stitch with a C, two 2 mm fire-polished beads, and a C **(figure 3, a–b)**. Continue working in RAW following the established color pattern to complete the row **(b–c)**, making note that two 2 mm beads are used in place of a 4 mm bead.
Row 7: Work a row using 2 mms **(figure 4)**. Each stitch should consist of eight 2 mms.
4 Continue working in RAW for the desired bracelet length (less ⅜ in./1 cm for the clasp), following the color pattern established in rows 1–7. A 7½ in. (19.1 cm) bracelet (with the clasp) repeats rows 1–7 twice and then repeats rows 1–6 once, but uses all Cs in the last row to keep the colors consistent.

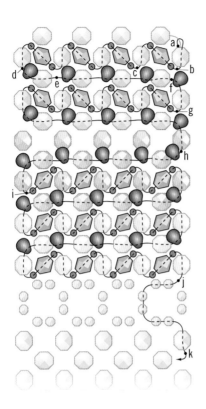

FIGURE 5

FIGURE 6

EMBELLISHMENT

1 With the working thread, sew around the closest thread bridge, and continue back through the 4 mm your thread is exiting (**figure 5, a–b**).

note If additional rows of RAW were added to the base for extra length, the bead colors in the illustrations might be slightly different. Just work as per the instructions, making sure to embellish the additional rows.

2 Pick up a 15º seed bead, a 4 mm bicone crystal, and a 15º, cross the RAW stitch diagonally, and sew through the corresponding fire-polished bead, going in the same direction (**b–c**). Repeat this stitch three times to complete the row (**c–d**).
3 Pick up a 3 mm magatama bead, and sew through the adjacent fire-polished bead in the same RAW stitch (**d–e**). Pick up a magatama, and sew through the next fire-polished bead in the same row. Repeat this last stitch twice (**e–f**). Pick up a magatama, and sew through the adjacent edge fire-polished bead (**f–g**).

4 Work as in steps 2–3 once (**g–h**), and then repeat step 3 again (**h–i**).
5 Work as in steps 2–3 twice, and then repeat step 2 again (**i–j**).
6 Sew through the beadwork as shown to get into position to add the next set of embellishments (**j–k**).
7 Work as in steps 2–6 for the remainder of the base, ending on step 5 (**figure 6, point a**). End and add thread as needed.

CLASP

1 With the working thread, pick up 10 15º seed beads and the end loop of the clasp, and sew back through the same 4 mm your thread exited at the start of this step (**a–b**). Continue through the next two adjacent 4 mms in the same RAW stitch (**b–c**).
2 Work as in step 1 to attach the remaining loops on the clasp (**c–d**). Retrace the thread path to reinforce the connection, and end the working thread and tail.
3 On the opposite end of the bracelet, add 12-in. (30 cm) of thread, exiting an end edge fire-polished bead. Work as in steps 1–2 to attach the other half of the clasp, and end the thread.

Crystalline cuff

Rose montees add shine and interest to this right-angle weave base made with Baroque seed beads. Top the cuff with Tiffany cups for an elegant focal piece.

designed by Dana Rudolph

MATERIALS

golden bracelet 7¼ in. (18.4 cm)

- **6** cups SS29 Swarovski Tiffany cup chain (white patina)
- **6** SS16 (4 mm) rose montées (Swarovski 53102, blue shade)
- **32** SS12 (3 mm) rose montées (Swarovski 53100, crystal AB)
- 3 mm Swarovski crystal pearls
  - **64** color A (bronze)
  - **36** color B (gold)
- **268** 6º Baroque seed beads (Miyuki 3953, gold)
- **1 g** 11º seed beads (Toho 279, color-lined mantique gold/crystal)
- **1 g** 15º seed beads (Toho 989, gold-lined crystal)
- **1** 5-strand box clasp
- Fireline, 10 lb. test
- beeswax or thread conditioner
- beading needle, #11
- flexible twisted wire needle, medium

TECHNIQUES

- beading fundamentals: ending and adding thread, square knot (p. 20)
- right-angle weave: flat strip, adding rows (p. 46)

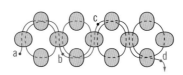

FIGURE 1

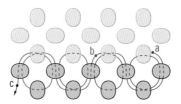

FIGURE 2

TIP Baroque seed beads have a special coating, resembling a pearl. The crepey ruggedness adds texture and reflects light.

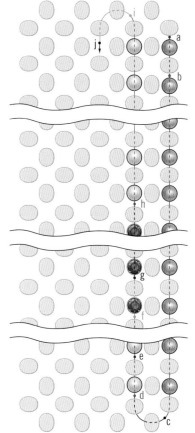

FIGURE 3

BASE

1 On a comfortable length of conditioned thread, pick up four 6º Baroque seed beads. Tie a square knot, and sew through the first three beads again to form a ring (**figure 1, a–b**).

2 Working in right-angle weave (RAW), pick up three 6ºs, and sew through the 6º your thread exited at the start of this step. Continue through the first two 6ºs just added (**b–c**). Continue working in RAW to add two more stitches using a tight tension, but sew through only one bead instead of two for the last stitch (**c–d**).

3 To add more rows, pick up three 6ºs, and sew through the 6º your thread is exiting in the previous row. Sew through the three 6ºs just added and next edge 6º (**figure 2, a–b**). Working

in a figure-eight pattern pick up two 6ºs per stitch to complete the second row (**b–c**). Continue working in RAW for a total of 28 rows, or to your desired length, ending and adding thread as needed.

EMBELLISHMENT

1 Sew through the beadwork to exit the end 6º on the edge as shown (**figure 3, point a**). Pick up a color A pearl, and sew through the next edge 6º (**a–b**). Repeat this stitch for the remainder of the base (**b–c**). Sew through the next two 6ºs as shown to start the next row (**c–d**).

2 Pick up a color B pearl, and sew through the next 6º in the row (**d–e**). Repeat this stitch eight times (**e–f**).

3 Pick up a SS12 rose montée, and sew through the next 6º (f–g). Repeat this stitch eight times (**g–h**).

4 Work as before to add nine B pearls (**h–i**). Sew through the next two 6ºs as shown to start the next row (**i–j**).

5 Work as before to add seven SS12 rose montées, and then add three SS16 rose montées. Remove the beading needle, and attach the flexible needle.

6 Pick up the end cup of the cup chain, and carefully sew under the chaton. Continue through the remaining cups, skipping the next six 6ºs below, and sew through the following 6º (**figure 4**). Remove the flexible needle, and attach the beading needle to the working thread.

7 Work as before to add three SS16 rose montées and seven SS12 rose montées.

FIGURE 4

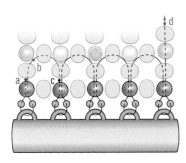

FIGURE 5

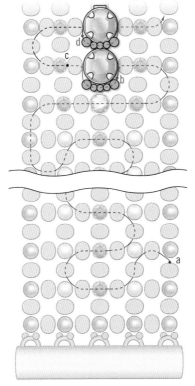

FIGURE 6

	6º Baroque seed bead
	3 mm pearl, color A
	3 mm pearl, color B
	SS12 rose montée
	SS16 rose montée
	7 x 5 mm cup chain
	cup chain side view
	15º seed bead
	11º seed bead

Sew through the next two 6ºs to start the next row.

8 Repeat steps 2–4 to complete the fourth row.

9 Work as in step 1 to add As along this edge.

note This bracelet is designed for a 6¼ in. (15.9 cm) wrist. Each row adds ⅜ in. (1 cm) to the length of the cuff. Add or omit rows as needed for the desired length.

CLASP AND FINISHING

1 Pick up an A pearl and a 15º seed bead, and sew through the end loop of the clasp. Pick up a 15º, and sew back through the pearl and the 6º your thread exited at the start of this step (**figure 5, a–b**). Sew through the next two 6ºs as shown (**b–c**). Repeat these stitches four times to attach each clasp loop, but exit the second edge 6º (**c–d**).

2 Reinforce the 10 rose montées on this end by sewing through the beadwork in a zigzag (**figure 6, a–b**). When reaching the cup chain (**point b**), pick up an 11º seed bead, three 15ºs, and an 11º, sew over the cup chain tab, and continue through the corresponding 6º (**b–c**). Continue through the next rose montée, three 6ºs, rose montée, and 6º as shown (**c–d**). Repeat these stitches to secure all the remaining cups and rose montées.

3 Repeat step 1 to attach the other half of the clasp, and end the thread.

TIP This project calls for SS29 cup chain along with SS12 and SS16 rose montées. If you're new to using cup chain and montées in your work, you might wonder what these codes mean. Montées and cups have two sizing systems: PP and SS. The abbreviation PP stands for pearl plate and refers to the size of a metal base with a hole. These plates were used for sorting, sizing, and pricing the pearls. Distributors passed the pearls through metal holes and categorized them by the hole that fit. The SS reference stands for stone size and overlaps with the PP system of measurement.

Funky fringe earrings

Dagger beads add some fun and movement to these embroidered Lunasoft earrings.

designed by Angie Mézes

mix it up

ALSO FEATURING

BRICK STITCH

& FRINGE

MATERIALS

earrings 1¼ x 2½ in (3.2 x 6.4 cm)
- **2** 18.5 x 13.5 mm oval Lunasoft cabochons (lavender)
- **2** 6 mm pearls (Swarovski, iridescent purple)
- **4** 4 mm bicone crystals (Swarovski, chrysolite opal AB2x)
- **14** 3 mm bicone crystals (Swarovski, fuchsia)
- **14** 5 x 16 mm CzechMate two-hole dagger beads (opaque luster green)
- **4** 2.5 x 6 mm mini dagger beads (metallic suede gold)
- 11º seed beads
  - **2 g** color A (Toho PF558, permanent finish galvanized aluminum)
  - **18** color B (Toho 221F, frosted bronze)
- **1 g** 11º Delica cylinder beads (Miyuki DB0455, galvanized dark plum)
- **1 g** 15º seed beads (Toho 84, metallic moss iris)
- **1** pair of earring findings
- Fireline, 6 lb. test
- beading needles, #11 or #12
- **2** 1½-in. (3.8 cm) squares of beading foundation
- **2** 1½-in. (3.8 cm) squares of Ultrasuede (tan)
- E6000 adhesive
- **2** pairs of chainnose, bentnose, and/or flatnose pliers
- scissors

TECHNIQUES
- beading fundamentals: ending and adding thread, square knot (p. 20)

EMBROIDERY

1 Apply a thin coat of E6000 to the back of a Lunasoft cabochon, and center the cab on the top half of a 1½-in. (3.8 cm) square of beading foundation. Allow the glue to dry.

2 Tie an overhand knot at the end of 2 ft. (61 cm) of thread. Sew up through the back of the foundation, exiting near the outer edge of the cab. Work in beaded backstitch around the cab: Pick up two color A 11º seed beads for each stitch, line them up next to the cab, and sew back through the

foundation. Sew up between the two beads and through the second bead just added. End with an even number of beads, and sew through the first A in the round, the foundation, and back up through the foundation and next A. Sew through all the As once more, down through the foundation, and continue up through the foundation next to the round of As on the bottom edge of the cab near the center **(photo a)**.

3 Pick up a 6 mm pearl, and sew through the foundation slightly behind

a

b

c

the hole of the pearl that the thread is exiting. Sew up through the foundation between the As and pearl, and continue through the pearl. Pick up a 15⁰ seed bead, sew back through the pearl, down through the foundation, and back up through the foundation near where the pearl and As meet.

4 Picking up two As per stitch, work a round of beaded backstitch around the pearl (**photo b**). Sew down through the beads and foundation. Make a half-hitch knot and end the thread. Carefully trim the foundation close to the beads, being careful not to cut any threads.

5 Glue the wrong side of the Ultrasuede to the back of the foundation. Allow the glue to dry, and trim the Ultrasuede close to the foundation.

6 Tie an overhand knot at the end of 2 ft. (61 cm) of thread, and trim the tail. Sew between the Ultrasuede and foundation, exiting the front of the foundation about 1 mm from the edge, hiding the knot between the two layers.

7 Work a brick stitch edging: Pick up two 11⁰ cylinder beads, sew up through both foundation layers one bead's width away from where the thread is exiting, and continue back through the second bead added. For each subsequent stitch, pick up a cylinder, and sew up through both layers one bead's width away from where the thread is exiting, and continue through the new bead just added. Repeat this stitch around the perimeter (**photo c**). When embellishing around the pearl, stitch 11 or 12 cylinder beads to this area.

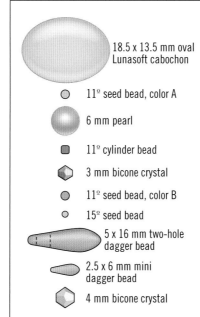

	18.5 x 13.5 mm oval Lunasoft cabochon
○	11⁰ seed bead, color A
●	6 mm pearl
▢	11⁰ cylinder bead
◈	3 mm bicone crystal
○	11⁰ seed bead, color B
○	15⁰ seed bead
⬥	5 x 16 mm two-hole dagger bead
⬭	2.5 x 6 mm mini dagger bead
⬡	4 mm bicone crystal

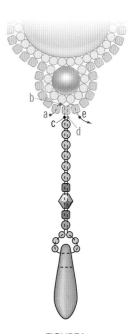

FIGURE 1

After adding the final bead, sew down through the first bead in the edging, through the foundation and Ultrasuede, and back through the first bead again. End the working thread in the edging beads.

FRINGE

1 Thread a needle on each end of 1 yd. (.9 m) of thread, and count how many cylinder beads are around the outer ring of the pearl. You should have either 11 or 12 cylinders.

2 Add the first fringe strand as follows

depending on how many cylinders are around the pearl:

If you have 11 cylinder beads: With one needle, sew through the fifth cylinder bead from the corner with the needle pointing toward the beadwork (**figure 1, a–b**), and center the thread. Continue out through the next cylinder bead (**b–c**). Pick up six As, a cylinder, a 3 mm bicone crystal, a cylinder, a color B 11⁰ seed bead, three 15⁰ seed beads, a dagger bead, and three 15⁰s. Sew back through the B and the remaining nine beads in the fringe strand (**c–d**).

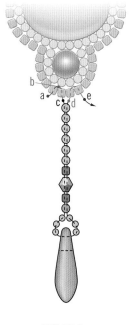

FIGURE 2

FIGURE 3

Continue through the cylinder your thread is exiting, and out through the following cylinder (**d–e**).

If you have 12 cylinder beads: With one needle, sew through the fifth cylinder bead from the corner with the needle pointing toward the beadwork (**figure 2, a–b**), and center the thread. Continue out through the next cylinder bead (**b–c**). Pick up six As, a cylinder, a 3 mm bicone crystal, a cylinder, a color B 11º seed bead, three 15º seed beads, a dagger bead, and three 15ºs. Sew back through the B and the remaining nine beads in the fringe strand (**c–d**). Continue through the cylinder adjacent to the one your thread is exiting, and out through the following cylinder (**d–e**). This will center this fringe strand between the two cylinder beads.

3 With each thread, add three more identical fringes on each side of the center fringe, except decrease the number of As by one for each fringe (**figure 3, a–b and aa–bb**).

4 On each thread, pick up an A, a B, two 15ºs, a mini dagger bead, and two 15ºs, and sew back through the B and A. Continue back through the cylinder your thread is exiting, and sew out through the adjacent cylinder (**b–c and bb–cc**).

5 On each thread, pick up an A, a 4 mm bicone crystal, and a 15º, and sew back through the 4 mm and A. Continue through the cylinder your thread is exiting (**c–d and cc–dd**), and end the threads.

ASSEMBLY

1 Identify the three top center cylinders in the edging. Add 12 in. (30 cm) of thread to the earring, exiting the right-hand cylinder of the center three. Pick up seven 15ºs, skip the center cylinder, and sew down through the next cylinder. Retrace the thread path, and end the threads.

2 Using chainnose pliers, open the loop of an earring wire, and attach it to the center loop. Close the earring wire.

3 Make a second earring.

TIP You may substitute the two-hole dagger beads with one-hole dagger beads and the mini daggers with Rizo beads or other small drops.

Secret treasure bracelet

Create a dramatic double spiral with a secret treasure hidden within the twists of the bracelet.

designed by Shirley Moore

TIP As shown in the purple bracelet, swap accent beads of similar shape and size to use whatever beads you have on hand.

BASE

1 On a comfortable length of thread, and leaving a 12-in. (30 cm) tail, pick up three 4 mm pearls to start the formation of the spiral core.
2 Pick up two color A 11º seed beads, an 8º seed bead, a drop bead, an 8º, and two As, and sew through the first three pearls added, going in the same direction, to form a "drop bead loop" on the left side of the pearls **(figure 1, a–b)**.
3 Pick up two color B 11º seed beads, an 8º, a 3 mm fire-polished bead, an 8º, and two Bs, and sew through the first three pearls added in step 1, going in

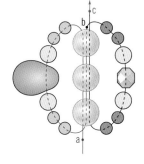

FIGURE 1

MATERIALS
green bracelet 8½ in. (21.6 cm)
- **46** 5 x 7 mm drop beads (mint gold)
- **48** 4 mm pearls (Swarovski, brown)
- **50** 3 mm fire-polished beads (transparent aqua gold)
- **5 g** 8º seed beads (Toho 4204, Duracoat galvanized champagne)
- 11º seed beads
  - **5 g** color A (Toho 2103, lime opal silver-lined)
  - **5 g** color B (Toho 221, bronze)
- **1** ¾-in. (1.9 cm) glass button (Czech)
- Fireline, 6 lb. test
- beading needles, #11 or #12

TECHNIQUES
- beading fundamentals: ending and adding thread (p. 20)
- spiral rope (p. 55)

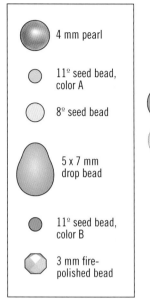

- 4 mm pearl
- 11º seed bead, color A
- 8º seed bead
- 5 x 7 mm drop bead
- 11º seed bead, color B
- 3 mm fire-polished bead

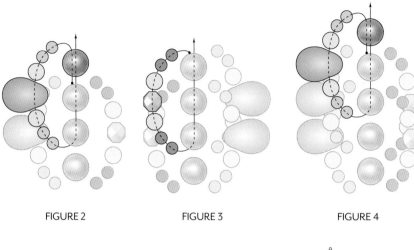

FIGURE 2

FIGURE 3

FIGURE 4

the same direction, to form a "fire-polished loop" on the right side of the pearls (**b–c**).

4 Pick up a pearl and the same sequence of beads as in step 2, and sew through the last two pearls in the core and the pearl just added, going in the same direction. Pull the thread tight, and push this loop to the left side of the pearls so it rests on top of the previous drop bead loop (**figure 2**).

5 Flip the beadwork so that the fire-polished loop is on the left. Pick up the same sequence of beads as in step 3, and sew through the last three pearls in the core, going in the same direction to form another loop. Push this loop to the left so it rests on top of the previous fire-polished loop (**figure 3**).

6 Flip the beadwork so the drop bead loops are on the left again. Work as in step 4 to form another drop bead loop, and push it to the left so it rests on top of the previous drop bead loop (**figure 4**).

7 Work as in steps 5–6 for the desired length, less 1¼ in. (3.2 cm) for the clasp, ending on step 5. The beadwork will naturally start to spiral. End and add thread as needed.

EMBELLISHMENT

1 Working toward the opposite end of the base, sew through the adjacent A of the end drop bead loop (**figure 5, a–b**). Pick up an A, and sew through the closest end A in the following drop bead loop (**b–c**). Repeat this stitch for the remainder of the base (**c–d**). End and add thread as needed. After the last stitch, continue through the remaining six beads in the end drop bead loop (**d–e**).

2 Working toward the opposite end of the base, sew through the first B of the adjacent fire-polished loop (**e–f**). Work as in step 1 to add a B between each fire-polished loop (**f–g**).

3 To add embellishment to the opposite side of each loop, sew through the core of pearls to exit the opposite end of the base, and repeat steps 2–3 on the other side of each loop.

CLASP

1 Using the tail thread, pick up a 3 mm fire-polished bead, a B, the shank of the button, and a B, and sew back through the fire-polished bead. Sew through the beadwork to retrace this thread path several times, and end the tail.

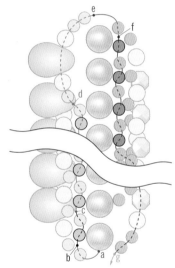

FIGURE 5

2 With the working thread exiting the core pearl at the opposite end, pick up a fire-polished bead and a repeating pattern of an 8º and a B 15 times, or enough times for the loop to fit comfortably around the button, and sew back through the fire-polished bead. Following the established thread path in the base, sew through an end loop and back through the end three core pearls. Retrace the thread path through the button loop several times, and end the thread.

Double chevron bracelet

Weave together two colors of chevron shapes for a layered, lacy look.

designed by Sue Sloan

BRACELET

1 On 2½ yd. (2.3 m) of thread, attach a stop bead, leaving a 12-in. (30 cm) tail. Pick up nine color A 9º or 10º seed beads, five 11º seed beads, and seven As. Sew back through the first two As added in this step to form a teardrop shape **(figure 1, a–b)**.

2 Pick up five 11ºs and seven As, and sew back through the first two As after the 11ºs in the previous stitch **(b–c)**. Repeat until you have 20 sets of five 11ºs along each edge, or until the band reaches the desired bracelet length less the length of the clasp bead and loop.

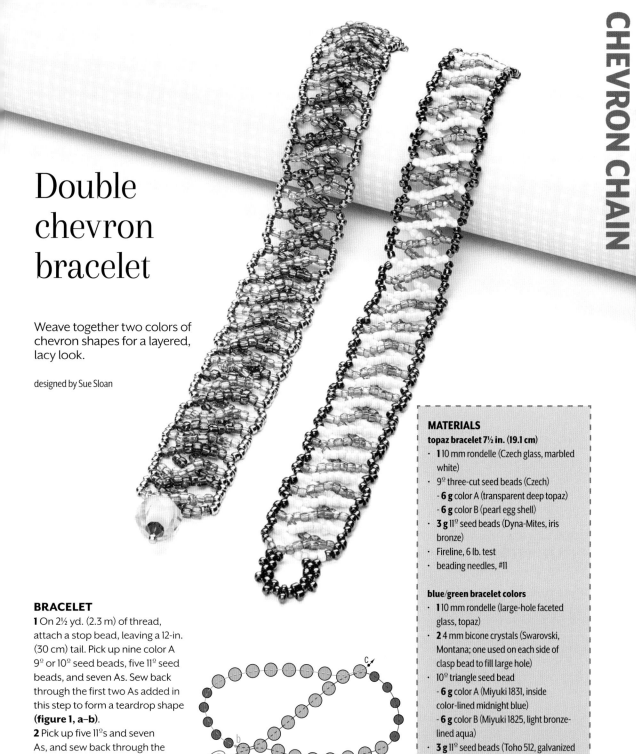

FIGURE 1

MATERIALS

topaz bracelet 7½ in. (19.1 cm)
- 1 10 mm rondelle (Czech glass, marbled white)
- 9º three-cut seed beads (Czech)
  - **6 g** color A (transparent deep topaz)
  - **6 g** color B (pearl egg shell)
- **3 g** 11º seed beads (Dyna-Mites, iris bronze)
- Fireline, 6 lb. test
- beading needles, #11

blue/green bracelet colors
- 1 10 mm rondelle (large-hole faceted glass, topaz)
- 2 4 mm bicone crystals (Swarovski, Montana; one used on each side of clasp bead to fill large hole)
- 10º triangle seed bead
  - **6 g** color A (Miyuki 1831, inside color-lined midnight blue)
  - **6 g** color B (Miyuki 1825, light bronze-lined aqua)
- **3 g** 11º seed beads (Toho 512, galvanized blue haze)

TECHNIQUES
- beading fundamentals: attaching a stop bead, ending thread (p. 20)
- peyote stitch (p. 24)

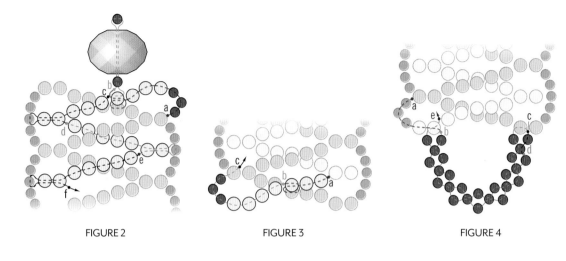

FIGURE 2   FIGURE 3   FIGURE 4

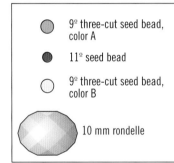

	9° three-cut seed bead, color A
	11° seed bead
	9° three-cut seed bead, color B
	10 mm rondelle

TIP You can substitute 11° seed beads for the 9° three-cuts or 10° triangle beads, but note that the finished bracelet will be considerably narrower. At just ½ in. (1.3 cm) wide, this would make a great wrap bracelet!

note Use medium tension, keeping your work lacy and flexible.

3 Pick up three 11°s and four color B 9° or 10° seed beads. Bring the Bs alongside the last color A stitch, aligning the fourth B with the fourth A. Sew through the A and the B as shown (**figure 2, a–b**).

4 To add the toggle bead: Pick up an 11°, a 10 mm rondelle, and an 11°. Sew back through the rondelle, the first 11°, and the B your thread exited at the start of this step (**b–c**). Retrace the thread path through the rondelle several times (not shown in the figure for

clarity), and exit the same B.

5 Pick up five Bs, sew through the center 11° in the nearest set of five, and sew back through the last two Bs just added (**c–d**). Note that these Bs lie over the last line of As.

6 Pick up seven Bs, and sew under the next line of As. Sew through the center 11° in the nearest set of five, and sew back through the last two Bs just added (**d–e**).

7 Pick up seven Bs, and sew over the next line of As. Sew through the center 11° in the next set of five, and sew back through the last two Bs just added (**e–f**).

8 Repeat steps 6–7 for the length of the bracelet,

alternating the "over-under" pattern and ending with step 6.

9 Pick up three Bs, and bring them alongside the first color A stitch, aligning third B with the fifth A. Sew through the A and the B as shown (**figure 3, a–b**). Pick up four Bs and three 11°s, and sew through the A your tail is exiting (**b–c**). Retrace the thread path through the first color A stitch, and end the working thread. Remove the stop bead from the tail.

10 To make the toggle loop: With the tail, sew through the three 11°s and two Bs in the last color B stitch (**figure 4, a–b**). Pick up 17 11°s, or

enough 11°s to fit around your toggle bead. For the best results, pick up an odd number of 11°s for the loop. **11** Sew through the second A in the first color A stitch (**b–c**). Pick up an 11°, skip an 11° in the loop, and sew through the following 11° (**c–d**). Work in peyote stitch around the loop, and end by sewing through the second B in the last color B stitch (**d–e**). Retrace the thread path through the clasp loop. End the tail.

Going in circles

You're going to love the stash-busting possibilities of this cute bracelet. Grab a few of these, a few of those, and a sprinkling of seed beads, and you'll be stitching chevron chain circles in no time.

designed by Julia Gerlach

MATERIALS
bracelet 8 in. (20 cm)
- 6 mm fire-polished beads
  - **19** color A
  - **7** color B
  - **6** color C
- **7** 6 mm glass pearls, color D
- **28** 3 mm glass pearls, color D
- 3 x 4 mm glass rondelles
  - **6** color A
  - **6** color C
- 11⁰ seed beads
  - **5 g** color A
  - **5 g** color B
  - **1 g** color C
- clasp
- Fireline 6 lb. test
- beading needles, #12

TECHNIQUES
- beading fundamentals: attaching a stop bead, ending thread (p. 20)

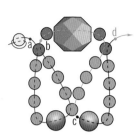

FIGURE 1

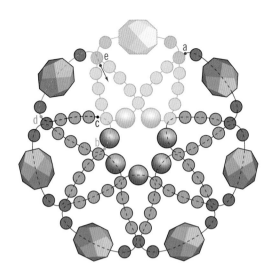

FIGURE 2

COMPONENTS

1 On 1 yd. (.9 m) of Fireline, attach a stop bead, leaving a 6-in. (15 cm) tail. Pick up a color B 11º seed bead, four color A 11º seed beads, a color D 3 mm pearl, and four As, and sew back through the B 11º (**figure 1, a–b**).

2 Pick up a B 11º, a color B 6 mm fire-polished bead, two B 11ºs, and three A 11ºs, and sew back through the first A 11º picked up after the D 3 mm in the previous stitch (**b–c**).

3 Pick up a D 3 mm and four A 11ºs, and sew back through the last B 11º picked up in the previous stitch (**c–d**).

4 Repeat steps 2 and 3 four times, then repeat step 2 again (**figure 2, a–b**).

5 To form the beadwork into a circle, pick up a D 3 mm, and sew through the A 11º adjacent to the first D 3 mm in the component (**b–c**). Pick up three A 11ºs, and sew through the last B 11º added in the previous step (**c–d**). Pick up a B 11º, a B 6 mm, and a B 11º, and sew through the first B 11º in the component (**d–e**).

6 To give the component more body, add a second layer of spokes: Pick up three A 11ºs, and sew through the corresponding A 11º, D 3 mm, and A 11º in the first layer of the component (**figure 3, a–b**). Pick up three A 11ºs, and sew back through the B 11º your thread just exited and the following B 11º, B 6 mm, and two B 11ºs (**b–c**). Repeat around the ring. Remove the stop bead, and end the tail, but do not end the working thread.

7 Repeat steps 1–6 to make two more large components (with seven 3 mms and 6 mms, as above) and three small components (with six 3 mms and 6 mms), varying the colors as desired or as follows:

· Make one large component with color A 6 mms and color D 3 mms. Use A 11ºs for all the 11ºs.

· Make one large component with color D 6 mm and 3 mm pearls. Substitute color C 11ºs for the B 11ºs and B 11ºs for the A 11ºs.

· Make one small component with color C 6 mms and 3 x 4 mm rondelles. Use C 11ºs for the B 11ºs and B 11ºs for the A 11ºs.

· Make two small components with color A 6 mms and 3 x 4 mm rondelles. Use A 11ºs for the B 11ºs and B 11ºs for the A 11ºs.

ASSEMBLY

1 Arrange your components as desired. Sew through an end component to exit at **figure 4, point a**.

2 Pick up three B 11ºs, a D 3 mm, and three B 11ºs, and sew through the two adjacent 11ºs at the edge of the component (**a–b**). Continue through the next three B 11ºs, the D 3 mm, and the following B 11º (**b–c**).

3 Pick up two B 11ºs, and sew through two adjacent edge 11ºs in the next component (**figure 5, a–b**). Pick up two B 11ºs, and sew through the middle B 11º, D 3 mm, and B 11º added in the previous step (**b–c**). Retrace the thread path a few times to secure the connection, and end the thread.

4 Connect the remaining components as in steps 1–3.

note Because some components have six 6 mms and others have seven, some of the connections will be offset from center, causing the bracelet to take on a wavy line.

5 Add 12 in. (30 cm) of Fireline in an end component, and exit an 11º opposite where it connects to the previous component. Pick up three B 11ºs, a D 3 mm, three B 11ºs, half of the clasp, and three B 11ºs, and sew back through the D 3 mm (**figure 6, a–b**). Pick up three B 11ºs, and sew through the two adjacent edge 11ºs in the component (**b–c**). Retrace the thread path several times, and end the thread. Repeat at the other end of the bracelet.

 TIP Choose three color families, and pair them in different combinations for a fun, casual look.

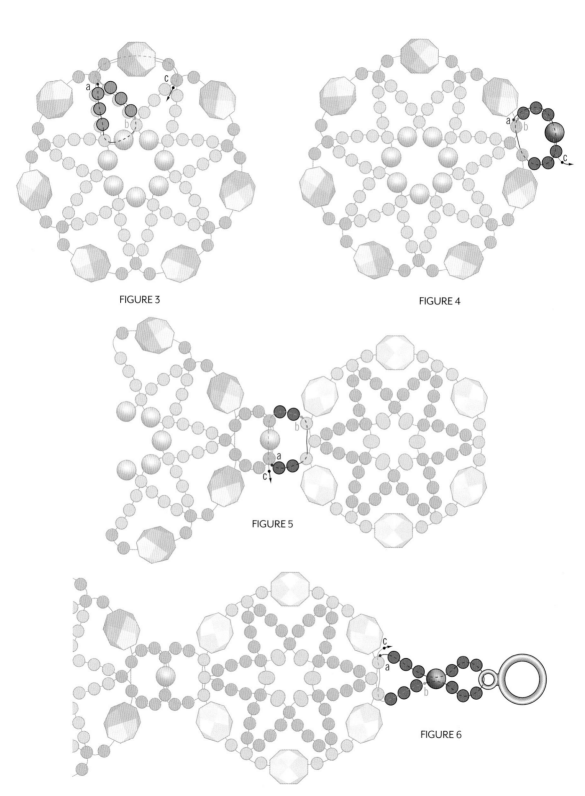

FIGURE 3

FIGURE 4

FIGURE 5

FIGURE 6

Caterpillar bangle

Bring a bangle to life with an easy tubular stitch teeming with textural embellishments.

designed by Cortney Phillips

ROPE

Maintain firm tension when beginning this rope. Once you've worked several rounds, the tension will maintain itself.

1 On a comfortable length of thread, pick up eight color A 11° seed beads. Tie the beads into a ring with a square knot, leaving a 6-in. (15 cm) tail. Sew through the first two As in the ring.

2 Pick up a color B 11° seed bead, and sew through the next two As in the ring **(figure 1, a–b)**. Repeat this stitch three times to complete the round **(b–c)**, and step up through the first B added in this round **(c–d)**.

3 Pick up two As, and sew through the next B in the previous round **(d–e)**. Repeat this stitch three times to complete the round **(e–f)**, and step up through the first A added in this round **(f–g)**.

4 Pick up a 3 mm magatama, and sew through the next two As in the previous round **(figure 2, a–b)**. Repeat this stitch three times to complete the round **(b–c)**, and step up through the first magatama added in this round **(c–d)**.

5 Pick up two As, and sew through the next magatama in the previous round **(d–e)**. Repeat this stitch three times to complete the round **(e–f)**, and step up through the first A added in this round **(f–g)**.

6 Repeat steps 2–5, until the rope is the desired length. As you work step 2 over the magatamas, make sure that the "bulb" of each magatama faces the outside of the rope and that your

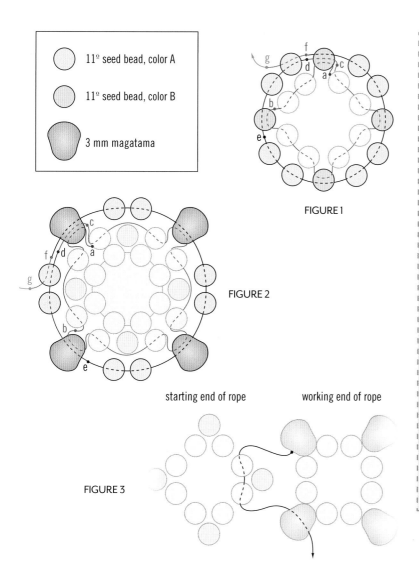

FIGURE 1

FIGURE 2

starting end of rope   working end of rope

FIGURE 3

Legend:
- 11° seed bead, color A
- 11° seed bead, color B
- 3 mm magatama

MATERIALS

yellow/cream bangle 7 in. (18 cm) inside circumference

- **160** 3 mm round fire-polished beads (Czech, topaz)
- **12 g** 3 mm magatamas (Toho 51, opaque light beige)
- 11° seed beads
  - **6 g** color A (Toho 762, matte opaque vanilla)
  - **2 g** color B (Toho 2110, silver-lined milky light topaz)
- **2 g** 15° seed beads (Toho 22C, silver-lined dark gold)
- Fireline, 6 lb. test
- beading needles, #12

purple/bronze bangle colors

- 3 mm round fire-polished beads (Czech, iris brown)
- 3 mm magatamas (Toho 703, matte mauve mocha)
- 11° seed beads
  - color A (Toho 221, bronze)
  - color B (F463R, olive metal matte)
- 15° seed beads (Toho F463, red purple matte metallic iris)

TECHNIQUES

- beading fundamentals: ending and adding thread, square knot (p. 20)
- chenille stitch (p. 58)

---

thread passes behind it. End and add thread as needed. For a bangle with a 6½–7-in. (16.5–18 cm) inside circumference (depending on individual stitching tension), work until you have about 40 rounds of magatamas.

7 Test the fit of the bangle, and add or remove rounds as needed. End with a round of magatamas, with your thread exiting a magatama.

note The starting end of the rope will resemble a diamond, and the working

end of the rope will look like a square, as in figure 3. The Bs at the points of the diamond should line up between the magatamas that form the corners of the square.

Sew through the A on each side of the corresponding B on the starting end of the rope, and continue through the following magatama on the working end of the rope **(figure 3)**. Repeat this stitch three times to complete the join, and retrace the thread path. End the working thread and tail.

EMBELLISHMENTS

1 Add a comfortable length of thread to the bangle, and exit a magatama.
2 Pick up a 15° seed bead, a 3 mm fire-polished round bead, and a 15°, and sew through the next magatama in the round. Repeat this stitch three times to embellish the round, and sew through the beadwork to exit a magatama in the next round.
3 Work as in step 2 for the entire bangle, ending and adding thread as needed.

St. Petersburg leaf earrings

These cute leaf earrings are quick and easy to make and great to wear in any season.

designed by Jane Danley Cruz

SIDE A

1 On 1 yd. (.9 m) of thread, attach a stop bead, leaving an 8-in. (15 cm) tail. Pick up five color A 11º seed beads, and sew through the second and third As, going in the same direction, so the fourth and fifth As form a new column (**figure 1**).

2 Pick up one A and two color B 11º seed beads. Skip the last B, and sew back through the next five beads in this column (**figure 2, a–b**).

3 Pick up a 2 mm fire-polished bead, and sew through the two As in the next column (**b–c**).

4 Pick up three As, and sew through the last A in this column and the first A just added, going in the same direction to form a new column (**figure 3**).

5 Repeat steps 2–4 eight times, ending with step 3 on the last repeat, for a total of nine fire-polished beads along the edge.

6 Pick up two As and two Bs, skip the last B, and sew back through the next five beads in this column (**figure 4, a–b**). Sew through all the fire-polished beads (**b–c**), pulling tight so the fire-polished beads snug up and the beadwork curves.

7 Sew through the six beads in the first column, skip the end bead, and continue back through the following five beads to exit the first bead in this column (**c–d**), tying a couple of half-hitch knots along the way. Remove the stop bead.

SIDE B

1 Pick up five As, and sew through the second and third A, going in the same direction so the fourth and fifth As form a new column (**d–e**).

2 Repeat steps 2–4 of "Side A" eight times, ending after completing step 3 on the last repeat (**figure 5, point a**).

3 Pick up an A, and sew back through the second and first bead in the adjacent column on side A (**a–b**).

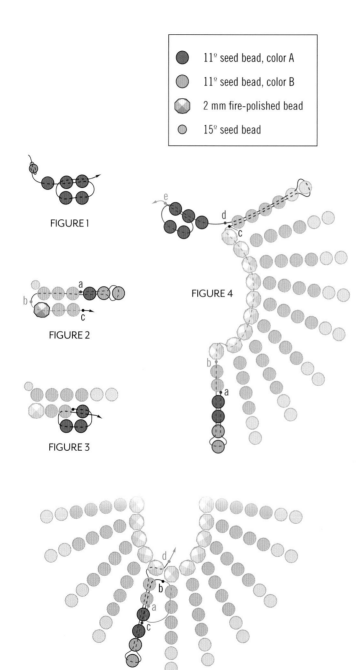

- ● 11º seed bead, color A
- ○ 11º seed bead, color B
- ◆ 2 mm fire-polished bead
- ○ 15º seed bead

FIGURE 1

FIGURE 2

FIGURE 3

FIGURE 4

FIGURE 5

MATERIALS
bronze earrings 1 x 1 1/4 in.
(2.5 x 3.2 cm)
- **34** 2 mm fire-polished beads (jet California gold rush)
- 11º seed beads
  - **1 g** color A (Toho 222, dark bronze)
  - **1 g** color B (Toho 1702, gilded marble green)
- **6** 15º seed beads color D (Toho 34, silver-lined smoky topaz)
- pair of ear wires
- Fireline, 6 lb. test
- beading needles #11

blue earring colors
- 2 mm fire-polished beads (jet black)
- 11º seed beads
  - color A (Miyuki 4518 opaque Picasso cobalt)
  - color B (Toho 1205, marbled opaque white/blue)
- 15º seed beads color D (Miyuki 2039, matte metallic royal blue)

silver earring colors
- 2 mm Czech glass pearls, in place of fire-polished beads (cerulean)
- 11º seed beads
  - color A (Toho PF558, permanent finish galvanized aluminum)
  - color B (Myuki 4220, Duracoat, galvanized eggplant)
- 15º seed beads color D (Toho PF558, permanent finish galvanized aluminum)

TECHNIQUES
- beading fundamentals: attaching a stop bead, half-hitch knot, ending and adding thread (p. 20)
- St. Petersburg chain (p. 64)

FIGURE 6

FIGURE 7

Continue through the first two As in the column your thread exited at the start of this step and the A just added **(b–c)**.
4 Pick up one A and two color Bs, skip the last B, and sew back through the next five beads in this column and the adjacent fire-polished bead **(c–d)**.
5 Sew through the adjacent fire-polished bead from Side A and the next six beads in this column. Skip the end bead, and sew back through the

following five beads and the fire-polished bead in this column **(figure 6, a–b)**. Continue through the next eight fire-polished beads on Side B **(b–c)** and the fire-polished beads on side A, tying a couple of knots along this edge as you go. End the working thread but not the tail.
6 With the tail, sew through the first A in the first column on Side B with the needle pointing away from the center

(figure 7, a–b). Pick up an A, three 15° seed beads, the loop of an ear wire, and an A, and sew through the A your thread exited at the start of this step, going in the same direction to form a loop **(b–c)**. Retrace the thread path several times, and end the tail.
7 Make a second earring.

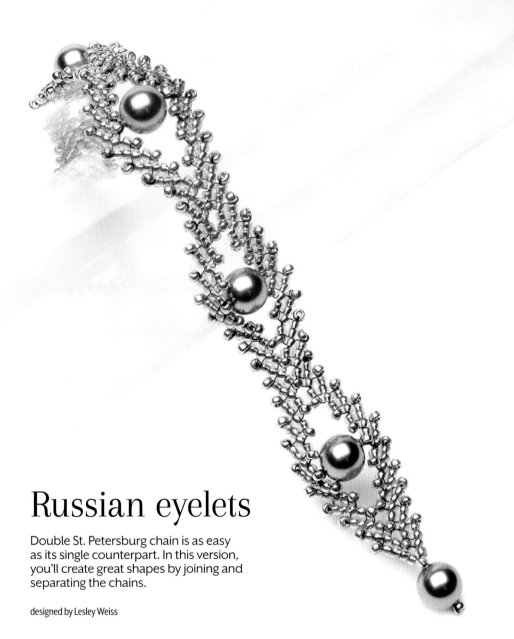

Russian eyelets

Double St. Petersburg chain is as easy as its single counterpart. In this version, you'll create great shapes by joining and separating the chains.

designed by Lesley Weiss

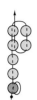

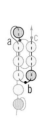

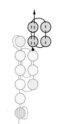

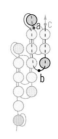

FIGURE 1   FIGURE 2   FIGURE 3   FIGURE 4

FIGURE 5   FIGURE 6

MATERIALS

bracelet 6½ in. (16.5 cm)

· **5** 8 mm crystal pearls
· 11º seed beads
  - **5 g** color A
  - **3 g** color B
· nylon beading thread, size D
· beading needles, #12

TECHNIQUES

· beading fundamentals: ending and adding thread, square knot (p. 20)
· St. Petersburg chain (p. 64)

FIRST CHAIN

1 Attach a stop bead at the center of a comfortable length of thread.
2 Working in St. Petersburg chain, pick up six color A 11º seed beads. Sew through the third and fourth As again, so the fifth and sixth beads form a second column next to them **(figure 1)**.
3 Pick up a color B 11º seed bead, and sew back through the next three As in the column **(figure 2, a–b)**.
4 Pick up a B, and sew through the two As in the next column **(b–c)**.
5 Pick up four As, and sew through the first two As just picked up, sliding the four beads tight to the existing chain **(figure 3)**. Pick up a B, and sew back through the last three As in the column **(figure 4, a–b)**.
6 Pick up a B, and sew through the two As in the new column **(b–c)**.
7 Repeat steps 5 and 6 until the chain has 38 Bs along each edge, ending and adding thread as needed. Secure the thread with a stop bead.

SECOND CHAIN

1 Remove the stop bead from the starting end of the first chain, and thread a needle on the tail.
2 Pick up an A, an 8 mm pearl, and a B. Skip the B, and sew back through the 8 mm and the next A **(figure 5)**.
3 Follow step 2 of "First chain" to begin the next stitch **(figure 6, a–b)**. Continue in St. Petersburg chain, but sew through the B added in step 4 of "First chain" to connect the stitch to the first chain, then sew through the two As in the new column **(b–c)**. Begin another stitch **(figure 7, a–b)**. Continue the stitch, but sew through the next center B in the first chain **(b–c)**.
4 Work steps 5 and 6 of "First chain" three times, causing a second chain to split off from the first **(figure 8)**.
5 Repeat step 5 of "First chain." Pick up a B and an 8 mm, and sew through the corresponding B on the first chain **(figure 9, a–b)**. Sew back through the 8 mm and the B so the thread goes through the B from both sides **(b–c)**. Sew through the two As in the new column **(c–d)**.
6 Repeat step 4 of "Second chain" to extend the split for three more stitches, then work two stitches as in step 3, joining the two sides.
7 Repeat steps 4–6 three times.

CLASP LOOP

1 Remove the stop bead from the end of the first chain. Work four stitches on each chain, forming a split.
2 On one chain, work a fifth stitch **(figure 10)**, then pick up two As and a B. Skip the B, and sew back through the two As just added and the other 11ºs in the column **(figure 11)**.
3 On the other chain, pick up two As, and sew down through the bottom two As on the first chain and up through the two new As **(figure 12, a–b)**. Pick up a B, and sew down through the next three As in the column and up through the last B and the column of As on the other chain **(b–c)**. End both threads.

TIP To make the bracelet longer, work three joined stitches instead of two in each repetition of step 6 of "Second chain."

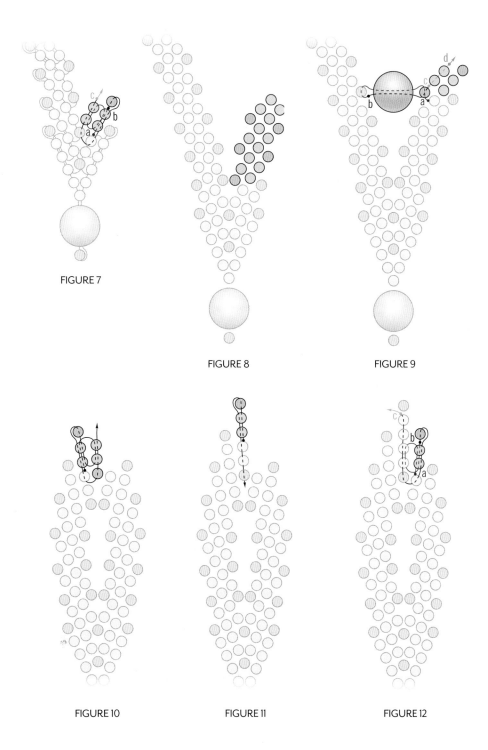

FIGURE 7

FIGURE 8

FIGURE 9

FIGURE 10

FIGURE 11

FIGURE 12

Fast finish

Make this entire bracelet on the loom by stringing seed beads onto the warp threads at setup time

designed by Julia Gerlach

MATERIALS
bracelet 7 in. (18 cm)
- **5 g** 11º Czech seed beads
- **3–4 g** 11º Japanese cylinder beads in each of 3 colors
- **2** magnetic clasps
- nylon beading thread, size D
- beading needles, #12
- loom

TECHNIQUES
- beading fundamentals: ending and adding thread, square knot (p. 20)
- loomwork (p. 66)

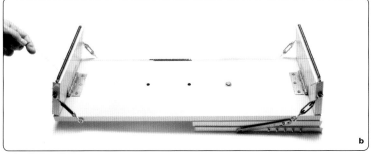

TIP **If you don't want to have to tie off 120 warp threads, put the warp threads to use by stringing seed beads on them between the panels. This cuts down the number of warp threads you have to finish off to only about 40.**

LOOM SETUP

1 Cut about 4 yd. (3.7 m) of thread, and tie one end to a hook or screw on the loom. Attach a needle to the other end, and pick up about 3¼ in. (8.3 cm) of 11º seed beads. Guide the thread through two coils on the spring at this end of the loom and two corresponding coils at the other end, positioning the seed beads between the two springs (**photo a**). Wrap the thread around a screw or hook at this end.

2 Guide the thread between the next set of coils, and pick up the same amount of beads as in step 1. Cross over to the other spring, guide the thread through the next set of coils on that end (**photo b**), and wrap the thread around the nearest screw or hook.

3 Repeat step 2 twice or until your thread is too short to span the distance between the springs. Tie the thread to the nearest screw or hook, keeping it snug.

4 Repeat steps 1–3 until you have 22 warp threads, each strung with 3¼ in. (8.3 cm) of seed beads.

PANELS

1 With your loom in a horizontal position, separate the beads on each warp into two equal groups. Push them to the ends of the loom.

2 Thread a needle on 2 yd. (1.8 m) of thread, and tie the end to the center of the left warp.

3 Following the pattern in **figure 1**, work the center panel in loomwork with 11º cylinder beads, ending and adding thread as needed. When the panel is complete, end the tails.

FIGURE 1

FIGURE 2

4 Working as in steps 2 and 3, follow **figure 2** to work the end panels, making sure they are snugged up close to the beads on the warps.

FINISHING

1 Cut the bracelet from the loom, leaving the warp threads as long as possible. At each end of the bracelet, end all the warp threads but two.
2 With a remaining warp thread on one end, exit the last row of the panel between the two beads at the edge. Pick up three cylinder beads, half of a magnetic clasp, and three cylinders. Skip the next five cylinders in the end row, and sew back through them **(figure 3)**. Retrace the thread path through the loop a few times to secure the connection, and end the thread. Repeat with the other warp thread remaining on this panel.
3 Repeat step 2 at the other end of the bracelet.

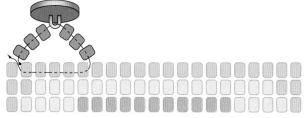

FIGURE 3

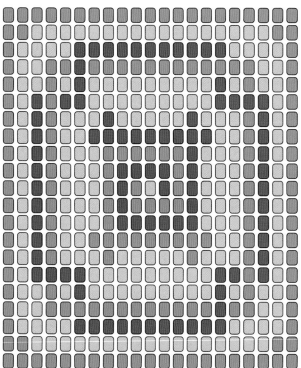

FIGURE 4

TIP Change the pattern for the main panel slightly in a teal, bronze, and blue version of this bracelet (see figure 4). If you want to design your own panels, go to BeadAndButton.com/graphpaper, and download the free graph paper for loomwork.

Braided bracelet

Discover the easy rhythm of bead crochet with this
bangle of three crochet ropes braided together.
Working with the tiny 11º cylinder beads may take
some time, but you'll love the detailed results.

designed by Olga Mihaylova

BRACELET

1 Measure around the widest part of your hand. To accommodate the braiding, each rope will need to be about one-third longer than your hand measurement. Mine were 8½ in. (21.6 cm).

2 Thread a beading needle on the color A thread, leaving the thread attached to the spool. String color A 11º cylinder beads to equal five times the desired finished length of the rope. I strung 45 in. (1.1 m).

3 Leaving a 10-in. (25 cm) tail, work five bead chain stitches. Insert the hook to the left of the first bead, and join the chain into a ring with a bead slip stitch.

4 Work in bead slip stitch until the rope is the desired length. Leaving a 6-in. (15 cm) tail, cut the thread from the spool, and pull the tail through the loop of the last stitch.

5 Repeat steps 2–4 with colors B and C, making the ropes exactly the same length.

6 Lay the three ropes next to each other with the starting ends all on the same side. Tape the ends together, and braid the ropes together tightly. Making sure the colors line up at the two ends, tape the ropes together at the other end **(photo)**.

7 Use the invisible join method to join the ends of each rope. Remove the tape, and end the threads.

MATERIALS

bracelet 3 in. (7.6 cm) outside diameter and 2½ in. (6.4 cm) inside diameter

- 4 g 11º Japanese cylinder beads in each of 3 colors: A, B, C
- 1 spool Gutermann polyester topstitching thread in each of 3 colors: A, B, C
- 1.5 mm steel crochet hook
- beading needles, #11
- tapestry needle, #26
- tape

TECHNIQUES

- beading fundamentals: ending and adding thread, square knot (p. 20)
- bead crochet: chain stitch, slip stitch, invisible join (p. 68)

contributors

Jimmie Boatright is a retired public school educator who teaches her original designs at Beadjoux Bead Shop in Braselton, Georgia. Contact her at dboatri931@aol.com or visit www. beadjoux.com.

Cary Borelli is an at-home jewelry designer/teacher in Las Vegas, NV. She can be contacted at CreationsByCary@aol.com or via her website, CreationsByCary.Etsy.com.

Janice Chatham began beading about 10 years ago after taking a beading class with her mother. She enjoys the calming and creative nature of the hobby. When she's not beading, she likes to volunteer at her local food pantry. Contact Janice at bighjh2@aol.com.

Lorraine Coetzee is a beading artist from Cape Town, South Africa, who designs patterns and tutorials. Her work has been featured in several publications. When she is not creating, you'll find her chasing after her mischievous dog, Mishka, who loves stealing her beads. Visit www.trinitydj.etsy.com or email her at trinitydj@tiscali.co.za.

Jane Danley Cruz is a former Associate Editor at *Bead&Button* magazine and the author of *Ready, Set, Bead!*, available through Kalmbach Books. Contact her in care of Kalmbach Media.

Cassie Donlen is a former Associate Editor at *Bead&Button* magazine. Contact her in care of Kalmbach Media.

Julia Gerlach is the former Editor of *Bead&Button* magazine. Contact her in care of Kalmbach Media.

Ryan Messinger is the creative force behind Just Breathe jewelry designs, which helps support the Pandamanda Foundation (he is Vice President). The foundation is dedicated to spreading awareness of Cystic Fibrosis and works to provide family and loved ones the comforts in a home-away-from-home while receiving treatments. Ryan's sisters, Amanda and Jessica Messinger, are the inspiration for these initiatives after they lost their lives to cystic fibrosis. Visit www.facebook.com/pandamandafoundation to learn more about his charitable work.

Angie Mézes is a full-time jewelry designer in Budapest, Hungary. Her favorite technique is bead embroidery. When she is not making jewelry, she spends her time with her husband and two kids. Contact her at redtulipinfo@gmail.com, www.etsy.com/shop/RedTulipDesign, or www.facebook.com/redtulipdesign.by.angie.mezes.

Olga Mihaylova is the owner of Koolkat Designs in Mt. Lebanon, Pa., in the U.S. For more information, visit her website, olisbeadwork.com.

Shirley Moore has been published internationally, and she teaches classes at her local bead store. You can contact her at shirleymooredesigns@gmail.com.

Cortney Phillips of Hickory, North Carolina, has been beading since 2010 and loves anything that sparkles. Contact Cortney at cortneyphillips@yahoo.com, or visit www.baublesbycortney.etsy.com.

Contact **Dana Rudolph** in care of Kalmbach Media.

Marla Salezze is a jewelry designer and bead-weaving instructor, and the author of *Learn to Stitch Beaded Jewelry*, available from Kalmbach Books. Follow Marla's beading journey and purchase kits for her beading projects at www.beadedbymarla.com or contact her at marla@beadedbymarla.com.

Sue Sloan started beading about 30 years ago when her son was small. She was fascinated with the way seed beads could be woven together to create intricate patterns and shapes. It was magical to her then, and it's still magical to her now. Contact Sue in care of Kalmbach Media.

Lesley Weiss is a writer, editor, and beader living in the metro Milwaukee area. She's the author of *The Absolute Beginners Guide: Stitching Beaded Jewelry*, available from Kalmbach Books. Contact Lesley in care of Kalmbach Media.

Gail Wing has been beading for 25 years and works at Eclectica. Beading is her passion. Contact Gail in care of Kalmbach Media.

Kalmbach Media

Create Gorgeous
Stitched Jewelry!

Discover 25+ stitching projects
you can make in one sitting —
four hours or less!
#67895 • $21.99

Showcase CzechMates beads in
20 stitching projects from Anna
Elizabeth Draeger!
#67887 • $21.99

Enjoy 25+ elegant stitching
projects with seed beads, pearls,
two-hole beads, and more.
#67882 • $22.99

Make 50+ beautiful jewelry
projects as you learn the ins
and outs of the most popular
bead stitches.
#67908 • $22.99

Create gorgeous dimension
and texture by layering beads in
20+ easy-to-make bracelets,
pendants, necklaces, and more.
#67906 • $22.99

Buy now from your favorite craft or bead shop!
Shop at JewelryandBeadingStore.com

Sales tax where applicable.

P34088